Supplement to

MANAGERIAL ACCOUNTING
Concepts and Empirical Evidence

SIXTH EDITION

Lawrence A. Gordon
University of Maryland

Executive Chapter Summaries (in English and Chinese) and
Solutions to Chapter Problems

Boston   Burr Ridge, IL   Dubuque, IA   Madison, WI   New York
San Francisco   St. Louis
Bangkok   Bogotá   Caracas   Lisbon   London   Madrid
Mexico City   Milan   New Delhi   Seoul   Singapore   Sydney   Taipei   Toronto

Supplement to
MANAGERIAL ACCOUNTING: Concepts and Empirical Evidence
Sixth Edition

1 2 3 4 5 6 7 8 9 0 DOC DOC 0 9 8 7 6 5

ISBN 0-07-354280-6

Editor: Elaine Manke
Production Editor: Susan Culbertson
Printer/Binder: RR Donnelley

TABLE OF CONTENTS

PART I:

EXECUTIVE SUMMARY OF CHAPTERS

<u>PART II:</u>

章节概述
EXECUTIVE SUMMARY OF CHAPTERS

PART III:
SOLUTIONS MANUAL

EXECUTIVE SUMMARY
OF CHAPTERS
English Version

EXECUTIVE SUMMARY OF CHAPTERS

Executive Summary - Chapter 1
MANAGERIAL ACCOUNTING: CONCEPTUAL
FRAMEWORK

This chapter provides an overview of the broad issues that are discussed throughout the text. It begins with the following definition of managerial accounting. *Managerial accounting* is concerned with the design and use of information systems that support managerial planning and control. Thus, the purpose of a management accounting system is to support managerial activities via a formal system of gathering, processing, reporting, and evaluating information.

Two broad issues of particular importance to managerial accounting are information and decision-making. Indeed, the entire field of managerial accounting can be thought of as being built on the pillars of information and decision-making. This chapter provides a conceptual framework for viewing these two issues. This framework focuses the reader's attention on the following two questions: (1) what types of decisions are managers making? and (2) what type of information do managers need to make these decisions? In answering these questions, a computer-based decision support system perspective is taken.

This chapter also explains the relation between managerial accounting and financial accounting. The role of economic principles and organizational design issues, in understanding and effectively utilizing managerial accounting concepts, are also discussed in this chapter.

Executive Summary – Chapter 2
PROFIT PLANNING: AN OVERVIEW

This chapter focuses on the process of short-term profit planning, with an emphasis on the overall role of management accounting systems in such planning. Profit planning is the process firms use to set profit goals. In its simplest form, the managerial accounting view of profit planning is short-term in focus and based largely on three concepts. First, profits are defined as the difference between revenues and total costs. Second, total costs are defined as being equal to the sum of variable and fixed costs. Variable costs go up or down with increases or decreases in the production level of a particular product or service. Fixed costs are those that remain the same for a specified period of time, regardless of the changes in the level of production. Third, the difference between revenues and variable costs is defined as the contribution margin.

The basic logic underlying the use of the contribution margin is derived from incremental analysis. If the additional revenues from selling additional units of a product (defined as incremental revenues) exceed the additional costs associated with those units (defined as incremental costs), profits (losses) of a firm will increase (decrease). In other words, where the incremental revenues exceed the incremental costs, there is a positive contribution (or increment) to the profit margin.

A positive contribution margin is a necessary, but not sufficient, condition for overall profits because total fixed costs also need to be covered.

To the extent that a firm's fixed costs are not covered, a loss will ultimately result. Hence, a positive contribution margin is not a guarantee that a firm will not lose money. This situation is referred to as the contribution margin paradox.

Contribution margin, which is really a subset of incremental analysis, is an important profit-planning concept. Relevant costs and sunk costs are two other important concepts that are germane to the discussions of profit planning. Relevant costs are costs that affect the decision under consideration. That does not mean that there are no other costs associated with the decision, but rather these other costs can be ignored when making the decision at hand. Sunk costs are costs that have been incurred, but are not relevant to the decision under consideration. The fact that certain costs are sunk, and as such irrelevant to a decision at hand, does not mean that these costs represent a poor investment.

In most firms it is reasonable to assume that the likely range of operations for specific products (including physical items and/or services) does not vary from zero to infinity. Within the relevant range of operations, it is assumed that accounting costs and revenues are linear. The management accounting view of profit planning uses this assumption of linearity to identify a target level of output. By dividing a product's contribution margin per unit into its fixed costs plus target profits, you are able to derive the target level of output for the product.

Most firms sell numerous products. In this more realistic situation, it is usually quite difficult to accurately separate the costs and revenues associated with particular products. However, if a firm were to sell multiple products in a constant proportion to one another, the simple profit-planning model can be applied in a modified form. That is, it is possible to think in terms of "baskets of product sold," where each basket includes one unit of the base product and a constant proportion of the other products. The contribution margin for the basket can be computed, and can then be divided into the total fixed costs plus target profits. Thus, the solution derived is in terms of the number of baskets of goods, which in turn can be converted to the required number of each different product to be sold.

The analysis presented in most of this chapter assumes certainty, in terms of revenues and costs. Unfortunately, most situations are characterized by uncertainty. One way to relax this assumption of certainty is to consider the firm's unit sales level as a normally distributed random variable. The probability that the firm will at least break even or earn a target level of profit could then be derived. Of course, the complexities associated with addressing uncertainty in profit planning analysis are not limited to treating the sales level as a random variable. Costs, for example, could also be treated as random variables.

A more robust way of considering profit planning is to view revenues and costs as being derived from economic concepts of demand and cost analysis. This approach results in non-linear revenue and cost curves. Although more rigorous analysis can be conducted, this approach to profit planning requires information on demand and cost functions that are usually quite difficult (if not impossible) to obtain. Thus, the managerial accounting approach to profit planning is commonly used by firms.

Executive Summary - Chapter 3
COST ACCUMULATION AND MEASUREMENT

This chapter focuses on the concepts of measuring and accumulating costs. The cost concepts discussed in this chapter apply to most organizations. However, for illustrative purposes, it is easiest to initially explain these concepts in the context of manufacturing firms that produce physical products. Accordingly, the chapter focuses on a manufacturing example. This fact notwithstanding, as pointed out in the chapter, the cost concepts discussed are applicable to non-manufacturing environments.

A good starting place when discussing cost accumulation and measurement concepts is to distinguish between direct and indirect costs. Direct costs are costs that can be directly related (i.e., traced) to the cost objective. Indirect costs (often referred to as overhead costs) are costs that cannot be directly related to the cost objective. Thus, in distinguishing between direct and indirect costs, it is necessary to understand the cost objective. The cost objective is the purpose for which costs are measured. Since a given cost can be associated with multiple cost objectives (e.g., to measure both the cost of producing a product and the cost of operating a department), it is possible (even likely) that a particular cost will be direct with respect to one cost objective and indirect with respect to another. Both direct and indirect costs may be variable or fixed.

To allocate indirect manufacturing costs, firms usually derive an applied overhead rate based on a factor called the cost driver (e.g., direct labor hours). The applied overhead rate is calculated by dividing estimated indirect costs by estimates of this cost driver. As the actual production takes place, the indirect costs are applied based on the overhead rate.

An applied overhead charge is used for indirect costs instead of an actual charge for a number of reasons. First, an applied overhead charge averages out periodic aberrations in indirect costs, thereby giving a more realistic charge to a company's products. Second, an applied overhead charge averages out periodic aberrations in the level of activity associated with indirect costs. Third, an applied overhead rate is helpful in situations where the determination of actual costs lags behind the production of products. A fourth advantage is that an applied overhead rate facilitates organizational planning and control.

Cost accumulation for a particular product can be accomplished through job order costing or process costing. Under job order costing, costs are accumulated by jobs. As a particular job is completed with respect to a given state of production, the costs associated with that job are accumulated and moved to the next stage of production. Under process costing, costs are accumulated by production processes rather than by jobs. Job order costing is most appropriate for accumulating the costs associated with custom made products, whereas process costing is most appropriate for mass produced products.

Absorption and variable costing systems are also important concepts to the discussion of cost measurement. An absorption costing system is one where both fixed and variable manufacturing costs are charged to the value of the inventory. In contrast, a variable costing system is one where only the variable manufacturing costs are charged to the value of inventory. Under a variable costing system, the fixed portion of indirect costs is treated as period costs and charged to the income during the period incurred. Effective managers use both absorption and variable costing methods in making their decisions.

To reduce costs associated with inventory (e.g., inventory storage, financing costs, obsolete inventory, and increased throughput time), many companies have pursued the goal of achieving a just-in-time (JIT) production system. A JIT production system is one in which the goods in one stage of the production-sales cycle are completed just prior to being needed at the next stage. A JIT system is not, however, problem-free. For example, a JIT system increases a firm's dependency on suppliers, which makes it more difficult for a firm to meet a sudden, unexpected demand. Therefore, both costs and benefits need to be considered before implementing a JIT system.

Some firms have used a backflush costing system. Backflush costing computes the cost of producing a product after the product is sold. This method is most appropriate when a firm has very little inventory. The drawback of this costing method is its lack of focus on cost management at the production level because the actual costs are not tracked through the production process.

Costs play a critical role in planning and control of profits. Therefore, managerial accountants have developed elaborate accounting information systems for accumulating and measuring costs in manufacturing and nonmanufacturing firms. One such system is a standard cost system, which is discussed in Chapter 4.

Executive Summary - Chapter 4
STANDARD COST SYSTEM

The major focus of this chapter is on a standard cost system. Under this system, both direct and indirect manufacturing costs of production are estimated. These estimates are referred to as standards and are used as the basis for product costing. In other words, inventories and cost of goods sold are valued using standard costs rather than actual costs.

When a standard cost system is used, managers reconcile and analyze variances (i.e., differences) between standard and actual costs at the end of the reporting period. Variances related to variable costs are based on the actual level of production. Hence, if the actual production is higher than expected, the total standard variable costs of production should be higher than originally estimated. Thus, the analysis incorporates a self-adjusting budgeting device (sometimes called flexible budgeting). In contrast, the fixed overhead variances do not include this self-adjusting device because fixed costs, by definition, do not change for different levels of production.

A standard cost system offers several planning and control advantages as compared to an actual cost system. First, standard costing allows managers to develop timely product costing information for inventory and financial reporting, which is especially critical for publicly traded companies with tight reporting deadlines. Second, standard costing information helps firms make pricing decisions. Third, a standard cost system averages out aberrations in various production costs due to periodic increases (decreases) in input prices or activity levels. Fourth, and finally, a standard cost system facilitates organizational control via its emphasis on analyzing differences between actual and standard costs.

A standard cost system is more appropriate for mass produced products because their average costs tend to be stable, within a given time period, from one unit of product to another. In contrast, one-time, custom products (or jobs) are not typically valued using the standard costing approach due to a lack of information necessary to make meaningful estimates.

In the early years of the evolution of cost accounting principles, most manufacturing companies used actual costs to derive the costs of their products. The next progression was to use applied rates for indirect costs. Firms ultimately implemented standard costing systems for direct, as well as indirect, costs. Recently, with the technological capability to quickly process data and the rapidly changing business environment, some manufacturing firms have gone back to using an actual cost system. Despite this increased interest in actual cost systems, most major manufacturing firms continue to use standard cost systems due to the planning and control benefits.

The planning and control benefits of a standard cost system are not limited to manufacturing activities. Nonmanufacturing activities can also benefit from the use of a standard cost system. For example, if a firm's marketing activities could be broken down into a cost per sales unit, such information would be useful for planning and control purposes. In the final analysis, the appropriateness of using a standard cost system is contingent upon the characteristics of a firm's products and its environment.

Executive Summary – Chapter 5
COST ALLOCATION ISSUES

Costs are allocated to a variety of objects, including products, departments, and divisions. The purpose of the allocation is to assign the appropriate costs to the object in question. Whereas direct costs can be allocated in a straightforward manner to the cost objective, the same is not true for indirect costs. In other words, as discussed in Chapter 3, indirect costs cannot be directly associated (or traced) to the cost objective. Thus, there are problematic issues associated with allocating indirect costs and these issues permeate nearly all aspects of cost accumulation and management. This chapter focuses on the following cost allocation issues: (1) single base versus multiple base approach to allocating indirect costs, (2) the allocation of service departments' costs, and (3) the allocation of joint costs.

The varied nature of indirect costs makes it unlikely that any one cost driver will provide an accurate and reliable allocation methodology. Therefore, most firms use a multiple base approach (often called multiple driver approach) to the allocation of indirect (overhead) costs. The primary goal of multiple base approaches to allocating indirect costs is to identify the appropriate factors that drive the costs.

Departments in a manufacturing firm are frequently distinguished in terms of whether they are production or service departments. Products physically move through the production departments during the manufacturing process. In contrast, service departments support the production departments and their activities are indirectly related to actual production (e.g., the cafeteria located within a manufacturing plant). Service departments also often support the activities of other service departments (i.e., there may be a reciprocal relation between service departments).

The total costs of service departments are indirect costs with respect to a firm's products and there are three basic approaches to allocating such costs. First, there is the direct method, which ignores the reciprocal relation between the service departments and simply allocates the costs directly to the production departments. The step method is the second approach that attempts to consider the reciprocal relations among various service departments in an intuitive manner. The costs of service departments are sequentially allocated, based on the degree to which service departments serve one another. The third approach is the reciprocal method, which formally (in mathematical terms) considers the simultaneity associated with the reciprocal service departments' costs.

Joint costs are the costs associated with an inseparable production process of two or more products (called joint products) and exemplify the issues associated with allocating indirect costs. From a planning and control perspective, it is often argued that joint costs should not be allocated. However, the allocation of joint costs is needed to assess the profitability of an individual joint product, to determine the inventory value of an individual joint product, and to derive the price for an individual joint product. The two methods commonly used by firms to allocate joint costs are the net realizable value method and the physical units method.

The difficulties associated with allocating indirect costs are not limited to manufacturing firms. In fact, all organizations face cost allocation issues. For example, banks need to allocate indirect costs to individual services and consulting firms need to allocate indirect costs to specific projects. The techniques discussed for allocating indirect costs within manufacturing firms can easily be modified for use in nonmanufacturing organizations.

Executive Summary – Chapter 6
ACTIVITY-BASED COSTING/MANAGEMENT

This chapter introduces the reader to the activity-based costing (ABC) approach to cost allocations. Activity-based costing is a two-stage, multiple base approach for allocating indirect costs. During the first stage, the activities that cause an organization to incur indirect costs are identified and the related costs of each activity are pooled together. In the second stage, the costs for each activity are allocated to the cost objective based on a specific cost driver (e.g., purchase orders and machine hours) associated with the activity.

An ABC system is easy to use and tends to allocate indirect costs more accurately than allocation methods based on a single cost driver for all indirect costs. However, opponents of ABC claim the method improperly treats all indirect costs as if they were variable costs and that ABC puts too much emphasis on the allocation of indirect costs. In the final analysis, an ABC system appears to be beneficial for some firms but not for other firms. Therefore, wise managers need to quantify the benefits of an ABC system over an alternative allocation system before agreeing to install such a system.

ABC is most properly viewed as part of a firm's activity-based management (ABM) system, which relates to the process firms use to manage their activities. The objective of ABM is to have an organization's activities performed in an efficient manner. Thus, to implement ABM, a firm must identify those activities that are managed efficiently. These activities could be used as benchmarks for improving other activities. The efficiency of an activity should be analyzed in terms of a cost-benefit analysis, and ABC can be helpful in this assessment.

Executive Summary – Chapter 7
PRICING DECISIONS

This chapter focuses on the way firms make pricing decisions and the effect of such decisions on the revenues, and, in turn, profits of a firm. There are many different approaches that can be used to make pricing decisions.

These approaches include marginal analysis, full costs-plus target profits, variable costs-plus percentage markup, and target costing.

Marginal analysis is based on the profit-maximizing rule, which states that maximum profits are derived by producing and selling at the point where marginal revenues equal marginal costs. This approach assumes that a firm's revenue and cost functions (in an economic sense) can be derived. In reality, however, it is extremely difficult, if not impossible, to obtain the information required to derive a firm's economic cost and revenue curves.

Full costs-plus target profits is a more practical approach to pricing decisions than the marginal analysis approach. Using this approach, the costs are derived from the accounting data and the goal is to satisfy, rather than maximize, profits. Prices under this approach are derived based on the sum of variable costs, fixed costs, and a target profit per unit of sales. Once the price is derived, the firm needs to assess market conditions (i.e., whether the market demand for the product will support the price). This method has three main advantages over marginal analysis. First, the method relies on accounting data, which is usually readily available. Second, a full costs-plus target profits pricing method allows a firm to work toward a profit objective, which is well understood by users of accounting data. Third, this method is perceived as being fair by policy setters.

Another form of cost-based pricing is referred to as a variable costs-plus percentage markup, which starts with variable costs and adds a percentage markup to cover fixed costs plus profits. The percentage markup is intended to incorporate both the fixed costs per unit and the profit per unit desired by the firm.

When discussing pricing decisions, it is interesting to revisit the concept of the contribution margin paradox discussed in Chapter 2. The idea

15

underlying the contribution margin paradox is that a product can be priced to have a positive contribution margin, while at the same time lose money. That is, a pricing strategy that generates a positive contribution margin, (i.e., prices exceed variable costs) does not guarantee that total revenues will cover total costs.

Target costing is used when there is a well-established market price for a product or a service. Under this method, the firm shifts its focus to managing costs, such that a desirable profit level is achieved given the targeted price. Although technically a costing concept, target costing is intertwined with pricing considerations. A logical follow-up to target costing as a method of managing costs would be to attempt to reduce the target cost in successive periods.

Pricing decisions are fundamental to the survival of a firm. The conceptual approach to pricing decisions is largely based on microeconomic concepts, with marginal analysis at the center. The principles underlying marginal analysis are not easily implemented at most firms. Thus, the pricing approach managers seem to follow is to combine cost based pricing tempered by market considerations.

Executive Summary – Chapter 8
FINANCIAL PERFOMANCE MEASURES

This chapter focuses on financial performance measures for firms, as well as their subunits. There are at least five reasons why financial performance measures are very important. First, managers utilize financial performance to allocate scarce resources. Second, stockholders and creditors make their investment decisions based (at least in part) on financial performance. Third, financial performance is directly correlated to a firm's ability to pay its employees and managers. Fourth, management incentive compensation is often based on financial performance measures. Fifth and finally, understanding the strengths and weaknesses of financial performance measures provides an important foundation for evaluating the strengths and weaknesses of nonfinancial performance measures.

At the subunit level, managers should be held accountable for a set of activities for which they have control. Thus, organizational forms of subunits are often structured around financial measures of subunit performance. The use of cost centers, profit centers, and investment centers are key examples of this point. A cost center is an organizational arrangement where managers are evaluated in terms of costs. A cost center can be evaluated in terms of comparing actual costs with expected costs.

Cost centers do not consider the value of outputs associated with the cost of inputs. Thus, many evaluate subunits in terms of the value of outputs relative to the cost of inputs through the use of profit centers. In profit centers, the costs of inputs are compared to the revenues generated by the subunit's outputs. However, profits alone do not represent the entire performance picture. Hence, a common approach is to treat subunits as investment centers and measure performance by comparing profits to the investment required to generate such profits. The accounting measure of a rate of profit per unit of investment is referred to as return on investment (ROI) and is computed by dividing profits by investment level. ROI is a historical measure, which considers only one period's rate of return, and it is based on accrual concepts of income.

As a measure of performance, ROI has several problems. First, ROI is not equal to a true economic rate of return, which is referred to as an internal rate of return (IRR). The IRR is equal to that discount rate which sets the future expected net cash flows from an investment equal to the cost of the investment. Although the IRR is a valid measure of efficiency and performance, the problems associated with measuring future cash flows limit IRR's usefulness. A second problem with using the ROI as a measure of subunit performance concerns the issue of goal congruency between subunits and the organization as a whole. That is, maximizing a subunit's ROI would not be synonymous with maximizing the ROI of a firm. It should be noted, however, that the same criticism would apply to attempts at maximizing the IRR of a subunit. A third problem with ROI is the fact that maximizing a subunit's ROI (or IRR, for that matter) is not equivalent to maximizing the value of the subunit.

Some firms have turned to residual income (RI) as a method of measuring subunit performance. RI is computed by deducting a capital charge from profits, where the capital charge is usually thought of in terms of the firm's cost of capital multiplied by the investments utilized to generate profits. As a performance measure, RI lies somewhere between profits and ROI. That is, RI provides a partial mechanism for considering the level of investment utilized in generating subunit profits.

Examples of measures of firm level performance are profits, earnings per share, ROI, and RI. These accounting measures of firm level performance suffer from many of the same problems that exist at the subunit level. Thus, it is often argued that firms should be evaluated in terms of market measures of performance. For example, many argue that stock market returns provide an important, if not the best, gauge of a firm's performance.

18

Measuring the financial performance of an overall firm and its subunits is a fundamental concern of firms interested in efficiently allocating scarce resources. Unfortunately, there is no single valid and reliable performance measure. In addition, firms need to customize their performance measures to reflect geographic locations, cultural issues, economic conditions, and overall corporate objectives.

Executive Summary – Chapter 9
NONFINANCIAL PERFORMANCE MEASURES AND FIRM STRATEGY

This chapter focuses on nonfinancial measures of performance, which are viewed as a complement to, and not a substitute for, financial performance measures. In general, these measures tend to capture a firm's relation with its customers, its business operations, and its growth potential.

It is often argued that nonfinancial performance measures predict a firm's long-term future performance and that financial measures reflect historic or contemporary performance. In other words, the former measures are often thought of as leading indicators, while the latter measures are often considered lagging indicators. A second argument associated with the contemporary concern for nonfinancial measures of performance is that organizations need to link their overall strategy with some nonfinancial, as well as financial, measures of performance. In this latter regard, the balanced scorecard is a report that links a firm's strategy to its financial and nonfinancial measures.

The nonfinancial measures considered in this chapter are product quality, customer satisfaction, productivity, and market share. Product quality is the overall dependability of a product or service. A key dimension of product quality has to do with the percentage of defective products sold to customers. Customer satisfaction is the attitude customers have toward a company's products. Some of the key indicators of this measure are the percentage of warranty work and the percentage of repeat customers. Productivity, another nonfinancial measure of performance, refers to efficiency. Productivity can be thought of as a ratio of outputs to inputs (e.g., physical units of output per employee hour worked). Finally, industry market share is often viewed as a key nonfinancial performance indicator by many of the world's leading firms. Market share is computed by dividing the sales of a firm by the total sales of the industry. Market share serves as proxy for long-term acceptability and, in turn, growth of a product or service.

Whether using financial and/or nonfinancial performance measures, there is no set formula that will perfectly measure firm performance. This fact notwithstanding, the key is to find a meaningful way to combine these two groups of measures. Unfortunately, finding the right combination is easier said than done. Indeed, there are unlimited ways of combining and weighting these two groups of measures.

Executive Summary – Chapter 10
TRANSFER PRICING

This chapter introduces the reader to transfer pricing decisions. Transfer pricing is concerned with establishing the price that one subunit charges another subunit within the same firm for the internal transfer of intermediate products. The total profits of a firm may be affected by transfer prices among subunits, despite the fact that the revenues of selling subunits are exactly equal to the expenses of buying subunits. The reason is that transfer prices may affect the quantity of intermediate goods produced and purchased internally.

There are two primary objectives associated with transfer pricing decisions. First, a transfer price should motivate subunits to operate in an autonomous fashion. Second, a transfer price should encourage subunits to pursue goals that are congruent with the goals of the overall organization. Under most circumstances, it is impossible to develop an optimal transfer pricing approach that completely satisfies these two objectives.

The three generic methods of transfer pricing discussed in this chapter are: (1) negotiated, (2) market-based, and (3) cost-based. A negotiated transfer price is one determined through negotiations between the buying (i.e. acquiring) and selling (i.e., transferring) subunits, without interference from corporate headquarters. To determine negotiated prices within the internal organization, subunits often begin by considering the way prices are derived in the external markets. Assuming that an external market exists for the intermediate product, a starting place for a negotiated transfer price will often be the amount the selling department could charge for the intermediate product via sales to an external market purchaser and the amount the buying subunit would have to pay for similar units from an external market seller.

A negotiated price could be difficult to achieve where profit sharing is involved. For example, there could be a scenario where one subunit is in a stronger internal bargaining position than another and, as a result, is only willing to agree on a transfer price that is unacceptable to the other subunit. In this scenario, an internal transfer of goods may not result, and the firm as a whole could be worse off than if such a transfer did occur.

A market-based transfer price is derived from the price charged by an external market supplier. When the external market for the intermediate product is perfectly competitive, the market-based transfer price method usually dominates all other methods. However, the application of using a market-based transfer price often breaks down when there are imperfectly competitive markets for intermediate products. These imperfections usually lead the internal selling subunit to argue for a transfer price that is higher than the average external market price, based on difficult-to-quantify factors like higher quality and shorter lead-times for delivery. In contrast, the buying subunit will usually argue for a transfer price that is lower than the average external market price.

A cost-based transfer price is derived from the costs of the intermediate product. If the selling subunit is being treated as either a profit or investment center, some form of cost-plus is used to set a cost-based transfer price. If the selling subunit is being treated as a cost center, then a cost-based transfer price is usually set equal to the full costs of the transferring department. There are several problems with cost-based transfer pricing. One of the key problems is that the selling subunit may have little or no incentive to be cost efficient. Thus, if cost efficiency is a firm's objective, goal congruency may be lost under a cost-based transfer pricing approach.

Differing corporate tax rates have a significant impact on transfer pricing. For example, high transfer prices shift profits toward the selling subunit, while low transfer prices shift profits toward the acquiring subunit. As a general rule, global taxes are reduced and corporate net profits are increased when subunit profits are shifted from high taxing countries to low taxing countries. Thus, firms often use their transfer pricing schemes to assist in minimizing total corporate taxes. However, most countries have tax laws that are designed to prevent unfair ways of shifting profits via transfer pricing mechanisms.

Executive Summary – Chapter 11
BUDGETING FOR CURRENT OPERATIONS AND CASH FLOWS

A budget is a formal plan for future activities, usually (but not necessarily) expressed in financial terms. Most firms prepare budgets for current operating activities, long-term capital investments, and cash flows. This chapter focuses on budgets for current operating activities and cash flows. A comparison of actual results with budgeted results provides control of organizations. Budgets also serve to plan, motivate, coordinate, and authorize company's activities.

The planning part of operating budgets focuses on the forecasting of the next period's normal operations in terms of the costs of the inputs and the revenues generated by the outputs. The forecast is usually based on a combination of past experiences and future expectations. Different budgeting approaches assume different degrees to which operating budgets mirror past activities. Incremental budgeting assumes existing operating activities are to continue into the future at one level or another. Under this approach, the budget consists of a base portion plus (or minus) some incremental (or decremental) portion. The base is that portion of the budget, which is assumed to remain constant. The incremental portion of the budget is that part, which is driven by changes in budget related activities. Incremental budgeting has been criticized because the base portion often includes activities that go well beyond their useful economic life.

One alternative approach to offset the above noted criticism of incremental budgeting is zero base budgeting. Under zero base budgeting, there is no base and the entire budget is evaluated on a cost/benefit basis routinely. This approach enhances a company's flexibility and adaptation to changes in the environment. However, the application of zero base budgeting could be extremely time consuming and its costs often exceed its benefits. Therefore, most organizations utilize a combination of incremental and zero base budgeting.

The opportunity to exercise control is a natural outgrowth of operating budgets. More to the point, differences (often called variances) between actual and budgeted financial results can be calculated and analyzed to make operational improvements. Budget variances are also used to evaluate managers' performance. If managers know that budget variances will be computed and used as evaluation devices, they will try to maximize their performance in terms of such variances. Of course, it is important to implement controls and policies that would prevent any unethical and illegal actions to achieve the budgeted goals.

While operating budgets motivate the behavior of employees in some fashion, it is difficult to estimate the degree to which employees are motivated by financial versus nonfinancial incentives. One nonfinancial aspect of budgeting that often motivates individuals is the sense of commitment to a common organizational goal. It is believed that the strongest commitment to achieving budget targets usually results when budgeting is a participative process. Another nonfinancial aspect of budgeting that motivates individuals has to do with an individual's desire for achieving specific individual goals.

Therefore, there seems to be consensus on the fact that successful budgets should establish challenging yet achievable goals.

Cash flow budgets assist firms in managing their current and future cash flow needs. The primary objective of the cash flow budget is to prevent cash shortages or excesses of cash. The cash flow budget is often prepared in terms of two basic steps. First, the cash excess (shortage) at the beginning of a period is determined based on the differences between the cash on hand at the beginning of the period and the desired cash level. Second, the cash inflows and outflows during the subsequent time interval are estimated. The cash inflows and outflows are typically organized in terms of operating, investing, and financing activities, which allows the cash flow budget to be linked with a company's budget for operating activities and its capital budget.

Executive Summary – Chapter 12
CAPITAL BUDGETING

Capital expenditures (often called capital investments) are intended to benefit a firm's activities for more than one operating period. Firms usually prepare a capital budget, which is a list of anticipated capital expenditures, on an annual basis. The process associated with selecting and controlling capital expenditures is referred to as capital budgeting.

There are two major phases associated with the process of selecting capital projects. The first phase is the identification of capital projects that are consistent with achieving the overall goals of the firm. One way to approach the identification process is to classify investment opportunities in terms of project types, such as mandatory, cost savings, and revenue generating projects.

Mandatory projects are externally driven, must-do investments. Cost savings projects relate to investments that reduce the cost of existing activities. Revenue generating projects are externally driven and relate to investments that either help to generate revenues from new activities or increase revenues related to existing activities.

Once projects are identified, the second phase of the capital budgeting process is to actually select the project(s) to pursue. Unlike the identification phase, this selection phase lends itself to a set of formal procedures. The techniques used in the selection phase are usually classified as either sophisticated or naive. Sophisticated methods consider the risk of adjusted discounted cash flows associated with capital projects, while naïve techniques usually do not. The net present value, profitability index, and internal rate of return are the most commonly used sophisticated selection methods of capital budgeting. In recent years, option pricing models have also been used for selecting capital projects. The payback period and the accounting rate of return are the most commonly used naive selection methods of capital budgeting.

Agency conflicts (discussed in Chapter 1) may lead managers to make less than optimal capital investment decisions due to their concern for short-term performance. In order to encourage managers to make decisions that would have a positive effect on the firm's long-term success, most major corporations have adopted long-term managerial incentive plans.

The control phase of capital budgeting is often referred to as postauditing. Postauditing is the focus of the next chapter.

Executive Summary – Chapter 13
POSTAUDITING CAPITAL INVESTMENTS

The focus of this chapter is on the control aspects of the capital budgeting process. The control of capital investments (often called capital projects) involves postauditing of such investments. In this context, postauditing refers to the assessment or monitoring of capital projects to determine whether they are accomplishing their intended purpose. This chapter concentrates on the objectives, process, and performance effects of postauditing.

There are several objectives for postauditing capital projects. First, postauditing provides a financial control mechanism. Both inflows and outflows of cash are monitored through postauditing. Second, postauditing provides input to future capital expenditures and helps a firm to improve its future investment decisions based on past experiences. A third objective underlying the postauditing of capital investments concerns overcoming the psychological and political problems associated with proposing and terminating projects. In other words, postauditing introduces a degree of accountability to managers for their decisions.

The process of postauditing should involve a comparison of actual results with anticipated results in a way that is consistent with the selection method. In addition, the regularity of the postauditing process needs to be taken into consideration. Empirical studies suggest that sophisticated postauditing of capital projects is significantly associated with the improvement of firm performance.

Determining the acceptable degree of risk related to a capital project is a problem that confronts many firms. Since there is a direct relationship between the expected return and risk of a project, firms not willing to take risks need to compromise in terms of the expected return earned from an investment. Postauditing helps firms manage the risk of their capital investments. Effective postauditing allows firms to identify projects that should be either improved or abandoned during the life of the project.

Unfortunately, the control side of the capital budgeting process is often ignored. Postauditing not only can help to weed out unsuccessful projects, but also can assist in the selection of future capital projects. The empirical evidence suggests that sophisticated postauditing of capital projects can enhance firm performance and, in turn, firm value.

Executive Summary – Chapter 14
MANAGEMENTS ACCOUNTING SYSTEMS AS AGENTS OF ORGANIZATIONAL CHANGE

The degree to which an organization survives depends, in part, on how adaptable it is to changes in its external environment. This chapter provides a conceptual framework for viewing management accounting systems as agents of organizational change in response to a changing environment. The framework emphasizes the proactive, as opposed to reactive, role of management accounting systems in facilitating organizational change. As such, it sheds new light on the link between organizational design and managerial accounting.

The argument that management accounting systems can, and do serve as agents of organizational change is illustrated through two specific areas of managerial accounting covered in earlier chapters of the book. In particular, it is shown that managerial accounting-based performance measures (e.g., residual income) and managerial accounting-based methods for allocating indirect costs (e.g., activity-based costing) provide excellent examples of how a management accounting system can serve as an agent of organizational change. These illustrations are grounded in conceptual arguments, as well as substantial supporting empirical evidence.

EXECUTIVE SUMMARY
OF CHAPTERS
Chinese Version

章节概述

章节概述：第一章
管理会计：基本概念

    本章是对全书内容的一个概述。首先我们需要了解管理会计的定义。管理会计的主要职能就是为管理层的规划和控制提供有用的信息。因此管理会计系统的目标就是收集，整理，报告和评估信息并用以支持和帮助管理层的决策。

    管理会计最重要的两点内容就是信息和决策。整个管理会计领域就建立在信息和决策的基础上。本章对这两个重点提供了一个概念框架。此框架着重于以下两个问题：（1）管理层需要作哪些决策？（2）管理层需要哪些信息来帮助他们作决策？针对这些问题，本章从决策支持系统的角度予以回答，

    本章还对管理会计和财务会计之间的关系做了阐述。关于经济准则和机构设置对于理解和应用管理会计概念的作用也在本章有所讨论。

章节概述：第二章
利润规划：综述

    本章重点讨论短期利润规划过程，并强调管理会计系统在此过程中的作用。利润规划指的是公司设订利润目标的过程。简单的说，管理会计的利润规划是短期的，并且主要建立在以下三个概念上：首先，利润的定义是收入和成本之间的差额。其次，总成本的定义是变动成本和固定成本的总和。变动成本会随着生产量的变动增加或减少。然而在一定时期内，不论生产水平如何变动，固定成本保持不变。最后，收入和变动成本之间的差额被称作贡献毛利。

    贡献毛利是从增量分析中衍生而来的概念。假如由于销售量的增加而引起收入的增加，并且增加的收入（增量收入）超过了相应的成本增加（增量成本），那么公司的利润（损失）就会提高（下降）。换而言之，当增量收入大于增量成本的时候，利润就会有所增加。

    正的贡献毛利是必需的，但并不足以保证公司在赚取利润，因为固定成本也必须计算在内。假如贡献毛利低于固定成本，那么公司会有亏损。因此，正的贡献毛利并不能保证公司赚钱。这种情况被称作贡献毛利悖论。

贡献毛利作为增量分析的一部分，是一个非常重要的利润规划概念。相关成本和沉没成本是另外两个与利润规划有关的重要概念。相关成本是对决策有影响的成本。这不意味着没有其它与决策有关的成本存在，只是在作当前决策的时候其它成本可以被忽略。沉没成本指已经发生的成本，因此对当前的决策没有影响。某些成本对于当前决策来说是沉没成本，但并不表示这些成本代表了失败的投资策略。

大部分公司（包括生产实物的公司和服务性行业）的经营范围是有限的。在相应的范围内，我们假设会计成本和收入是线性的。在管理会计的利润规划中，我们利用这个线性假设来确订目标生产量。目标生产量等于固定成本加上目标利润然后除以单位贡献毛利。

大部分公司出售多种产品。现实是，通常很难正确区分跟某一特定产品相关的成本和收入。然而，假如公司按固定比例出售各个产品，我们可以对以上简单的利润规划模型稍加修正。我们可以用"产品篮"来考虑这个问题，每个篮子中包括了一单位基本产品和固定比例的其它产品。我们可以计算每个"产品篮"的贡献毛利，然后用总变动成本和目标利润之和除以此贡献毛利，从而得到目标生产量。但此目标生产量也以"篮"为单位。我们需要再把它转换成各个不同产品的生产量。

大部分章节的分析都假设收入和成本是确定的。可是，大多数的情况是收入和成本都是不确定的。我们可以放松"确定"假设，假定公司的单位销售额是正态分布的。从而推导出公司收入和成本持平或赚取目标利润的可能性。当在利润规划分析中引入"不确定"时，我们不仅可以假设销售额是一个随机变量，而且还可以假设成本也是随机变量。

另外一个更可靠的方法是将收入和成本看作是从需求和成本分析的经济概念中衍生而来的。这种方式下的收入和成本是非线性的。虽然此法的收入和成本分析更严谨，但这种利润规划方式要求获取需求和成本方程的信息，而这些信息通常很难获得。因此，管理会计的利润规划方式更常用。

章节概述：第三章
成本累计和估算

本章的重点是对成本进行累计和估算。虽然本章对成本的定义适用于大多数机构，为了简化说明，我们先讨论制造业公司，相应本章的例子也是着重于制造业公司。但事实上，本章讨论的成本概念也适用于非制造业机构。

当讨论成本累计和成本估算时，首先我们要区分直接成本和间接成本。直接成本与成本对象直接相关（或可以直接追溯到成本对象）。间接成本（间接制造费用）并不与成本对象直接相关。因此，为了区分直接和间接成本，我们首先必要了解成本对象。成本对象是进行成本估算的原因。由于某一成本可能会与多个成本对象相关（例如同时估算某个产品的成本和某个部门的成本），因此某一特定成本有可能与某一成本对象直接相关但与另一成本对象间接相关。直接成本和间接成本可以是变动成本也可以是固定成本。

为了分摊间接制造费用，公司通常会计算一个基于成本动因（例如直接劳动时间）基础上的间接成本分配率。间接成本分配率等于间接成本除以成本动因。生产开始以后，公司可以用间接成本分配率来分摊间接成本。

出于以下几个原因，公司选择用分配率来分摊间接成本，而不是直接衡量实际成本。第一，间接成本分摊平均了间接成本的季节性波动，因此产品成本估算更加合理。第二，间接产品分摊平均了与间接成本相关的生产水平的季节性波动。第三，当实际成本的确定滞后于产品生产时，间接成本分摊尤为重要。第四，间接成本分摊有利于机构的规划和控制。

我们可以用订单成本计算法或分步成本计算法来对某一特定产品进行成本累计。订单成本计算法中，成本按订单累计。当某一特定的订单完成时，相应的成本会被累计，然后进行生产的下一个程序。分步成本计算法中，成本按照生产步骤而不是订单累计。订单成本计算法适用于客户化产品，而分步成本计算法适用于批量生产型产品。

摊配成本计算法和变动成本计算法也是两种估算产品成本的重要方法。摊配成本计算法将固定生产成本和变动生产成本都计算到存货里。与之相反，变动成本计算法只将变动生产成本算进存货里。在变动成本法中，间接成本中的固定成本会当作期间成本处理并从当期的收入中减掉。经验丰富的经理人员在作决策的时候会同时运用两种方法。

为了减少与存货相关的费用（例如存货储存，融资成本，陈旧存货和产销时间增加），很多公司追求达到准时生产（Just-In-Time）的目标。准时生产的生产方式是指在产销循环中，每个环节只恰恰在下一个环节需要时完成生产。但准时生产的生产方式也不是没有问题的。比如，准时生产的生产方式提高了公司对供给方的依赖，公司会很难满足临时需求。因此，在公司采用准时生产的生产方式之前，必须同时考虑到准时生产方式的成本和收益。

有些公司采用倒冲法来计算产品成本。倒冲法在产品销售之后再计算产品的成本。这种方式适合于存货较少的公司。这种方法的缺点是在生产阶段缺乏对成本的管理因为在生产阶段无法知道产品的实际成本。

成本在利润的规划和控制中起到了很重要的作用。因此，管理会计人员研究出了很多精细的会计信息系统来累计和估算制造业和非制造业公司的成本。在第四章中我们会讨论到其中的一个信息系统-标准成本系统。

章节概述：第四章
标准成本系统

本章的重点是标准成本系统。此系统首先需要估算直接成本和间接成本。这些估计值被称作标准并且用作产品成本计算的基础。换而言之，存货和销售成本是用标准成本而不是用实际成本来衡量。

当使用标准成本系统时，公司在财务报告年度的末期，会计算和分析标准成本和实际成本之间的差额。标准变动成本和实际变动成本之间差额的计算是建立在实际生产水平的基础上的。当实际生产水平高于预期生产水平时，标准变动成本也应随之提高。因此，变动成本分析涉及到预算的自我调节（又称弹性预算）。而固定成本的差额并不涉及预算的自我调节，因为当生产水平变动时，固定成本应保持不变。

标准成本系统相对于实际成本系统在规划和控制方面有如下优势。第一，标准成本系统可以及时提供存货的成本信息和财务报告，对于有严格财务报告期限的上市公司来说，这点尤为重要。第二，标准成本信息能帮助公司制定产品价格。第三，标准成本系统平均了产品成本由于投入品和生产水平季节性增加（减少）而引起的波动。最后，标准成本系统强调对于实际成本和标准成本之间差距的分析，因此有利于企业内部控制。

标准成本系统更适于批量生产的企业，因为在一定的时期内，这些企业产品的平均成本比较稳定。相反，客户化产品通常不会用标准成本系统，因为缺乏估算标准成本的必要信息。

在成本会计准则演变的早期，大部分的制造业公司都用实际成本来计算产品成本。然后发展到用间接成本分配率来计算成本。最终，公司采用标准成本系统来衡量直接和间接成本。近来，由于快速数据处理技术的提高和瞬息万变的商业环境，有些制造业公司重新选择使用实际成本系统。虽然人们对实际成本系统的兴趣有所增加，但因为标准成本系统在规划和控制方面的优势，大部分公司还是继续使用标准成本系统。

标准成本系统在规划和控制方面的优点并不限于生产性行为。非生产性行为也能从标准成本系统中获益。例如，假如一家公司的市场营销行为能以单位成本计算，这些成本将会对企业的经营规划和控制起到很大的作用。最后，是否使用标准成本系统取决于公司产品的特点以及经营环境。

章节概述：第五章
成本分摊

将间接成本摊派至成本对象，包括产品，部门，作业等，称为成本分摊。成本分摊的目的是将成本合理的分配给成本对象。虽然，直接成本很容易分摊给成本对象，但间接成本分摊却很困难。如第三章中所述，间接成本并不与成本对象直接相关（或能直接追溯到成本对象）。因此，对间接成本分摊所存在的问题的讨论贯穿了整个成本累计和管理的各个方面。本章主要讨论关于间接成本分摊的如下三点：第一，单基础或多基础分摊。第二，服务部门成本的分摊。第三，联合成本的分摊。

间接成本的各种特性决定了只用一种成本动因来分配间接成本难以做到准确和可靠。因此，大部分公司使用多个成本分摊基础（或多个成本动因）来分摊间接成本。使用多个成本分摊基础的主要目的是为了确定导致成本产生的各个因素。

制造业公司通常分为生产部门和服务部门。在生产部门中，各个生产流程都有实物产品存在。服务部门是对生产部门进行支持，因此并不与实际生产直接相关（例如，工厂的食堂）。服务部门也会对其它服务部门的活动提供支持（服务部门之间可能会有相互的关系）。

服务部门的总成本对于公司的生产是间接成本，有三种方法来分摊这种间接成本。第一种是直接分摊法，这种方法不考虑服务部门之间的相互关系，将成本直接分摊给生产部门。第二种是逐减分摊法，此法是按各个部门提供其它部门服务多少的顺序来分摊成本。因此，此法考虑到了不同服务部门之间相互提供服务的可能性。第三种是交互分摊法，此法考虑到了各个服务部门相互提供服务的同时性。

联合成本是在共同生产两种或更多产品（联产品）的过程中产生的成本，也是间接成本分摊的一个例子。从规划和控制的角度来说，不应该分摊联合成本。然而，为了计算单个联产品的利润，确定单个联产品的存货价值和对单个联产品定价，必须对联合成本进行分摊。公司通常用变现净值法和实物单位法来分摊联合成本。

并非只有制造业公司会面临分摊间接成本的困难。所有的组织都会遇到分摊间接成本的问题。例如，银行需要将间接成本分摊给单个服务公司。咨询公司也需要将间接成本分摊给各个具体项目。本章讨论的制造业公司分摊间接成本的方法改动后也适于非制造业公司。

章节概述：第六章
作业基础成本法/管理

本章为读者介绍作业基础成本分摊法（Activity Based Costing，简称ABC）。作业基础成本法是一个两步骤，多基础的成本分摊方法。第一步，确定导致成本产生的每项作业并将与每项作业相关的成本归于一个成本库。第二步，每项作业的成本按相关的成本动因（例如购买单或机器时间）分摊到成本对象。

ABC 系统容易使用，并且能比只使用单个成本动因的方法更准确的分摊间接成本。然而 ABC 的反对者认为这种方法假定所有的间接成本都是变动成本，并且太过于强调对间接成本的分摊。ABC 系统只是对某些公司来说更有用，而不是对所有的公司都适用。精明的管理层需要量化ABC 系统与其它系统的相对收益，然后决定是否该使用 ABC 系统。

ABC 系统应该被视为公司作业基础管理（Activity Based Management，简称 ABM）的一部分，公司作业基础管理指的是公司管理作业的过程。ABM 的目的是促使公司有效率的完成作业。因此，当应用ABM 的时候，公司必须确认出哪些是高效率作业。然后将这些高效率作业做为改进其他作业的标准。我们应该用成本收益法来分析作业的效率，而 ABC 在这方面是一个有效的工具。

章节概述：第七章
定价决策

本章的重点是公司的定价决策和这些决策对收入及利润的影响。有很多方法可以用来做定价决策。这些方法包括了边际分析法，全部成本加成法，变动成本加成法，目标成本定价法。

边际分析法是建立在利润最大化的准则之上的，当产品的生产和销售使得边际收入与边际成本相等时，利润可达到最大化。这种方法假定我们可以推导出公司的收入和成本方程（经济意义上的）。但现实中，获取足够的信息来推算公司的经济成本和收入曲线即使不是不可能的，也是极端困难的。

全部成本加成法与边际分析法相比更实用。这种方法首先需要从会计数据中导出产品成本，然后在此基础上制定一个满足目标利润而不是最大化利润的价格。因此价格等于单位变动成本，固定成本和目标利润的总和。一旦价格确定，公司需要对市场作评估（例如市场需求是否能支持这个价格）。本法与边际分析法相比有三个优点。第一，此法只需要使用会计数据，而会计数据唾手可得。第二，完全成本法允许公司确立易于理解的利润目标，并向之努力。第三，这种方法比较公平。

另一种成本定价法是变动成本加成法。这种方法首先从变动成本开始，然后在此基础上加一个百分比来抵消固定成本并让公司赚取目标利润。

当讨论产品定价时，我们有必要再回想一下第二章所说的贡献毛利悖论。贡献毛利悖论是说公司设定的价格可以带来正的贡献毛利但负的利润。因此，能给公司带来正的贡献毛利（或者价格超过变动成本）的价格策略并不能保证总收入超过总成本。

目标成本方法适用于当某种产品或服务存在市场价格的时候。因此公司的重心就要转移到控制成本上，这样才能在给定目标价格下赚取到目标利润。虽然目标成本方法从字面上来看只是一个成本概念，但它其实是与定价策略密切相关的。目标成本方法可以通过在后续年度内降低目标成本来对成本进行管理。

定价决策与公司的生存密切相关。以边际分析为中心，定价策略其实是一个建立在微观经济基础上的概念。边际分析的准则在大多数公司中都不容易实现。因此，一般公司的定价策略都会结合成本定价和市场考虑。

章节概述：第八章
财务业绩指标

本章的重点是公司和公司部门的财务业绩指标。最少有五点内容可以说明为什么财务业绩指标如此重要。第一，管理层可以根据财务业绩指标来分配稀缺资源。第二，股东和债权人可以根据财务业绩指标来决定投资策略。第三，财务业绩指标与公司对雇员和经理付薪酬的能力直接相关。第四，经理的红利也经常建立在财务业绩指标的基础上。第五，了解财务业绩指标的优缺点为评价非财务业绩指标的优缺点提供了重要的基础。

在部门级别，经理应该为他们掌握之下的部门作业负责。因此，部门的组织形式通常是以部门的财务业绩指标为架构的。成本中心，利润中心和投资中心概念的使用就很好的说明了这点。成本中心的业绩是用成本来评估的，可以通过比较实际成本和预算成本来评估成本中心的业绩。

成本中心不考虑与成本投入相关的产出价值。然而对利润中心的业绩评估，公司需要考虑到与投入成本相对应的产出价值。或者说，需要比较利润中心的产出收入和投入成本。然而，单单利润并不能衡量公司的整个业绩。为了衡量公司的整个业绩，常用的方法是通过比较利润和投资来评估投资中心的业绩。单位投资的利润在会计中被称作投资回报率（Return On Investment，简称 ROI），等于利润除以投资额。ROI 是一个建立在实际收入概念上并只考虑单期回报的历史指标。

ROI 作为业绩指标有几个不足之处。首先，ROI 并不等于真实的经济回报率—内部收益率（Internal Rate of Return，简称 IRR）。IRR 等于使投资净现值为零的折现率。虽然 IRR 是一个衡量效率和业绩的有效方法，但由于对未来现金流的衡量有时会有困难，因此限制了 IRR 的使用。第二，ROI 作为部门业绩指标可能会破坏部门和企业的目标一致性。最大化部门 ROI 并不等于最大化整个公司的 ROI。值得注意的是，IRR 也存在同样的问题。第三，最大化部门的 ROI（或 IRR）不等于最大化部门的价值。

有些公司转而使用剩余收益（Residual Income，简称 RI）来衡量部门业绩。RI 等于利润减去资本设算利息，其中资本设算利息等于公司的资本成本乘以投资额。作为业绩指标，RI 介于利润和 ROI 之间。RI 为考虑产生部门利润所使用的投资提供了一定的机制。

公司级别的业绩指标有利润，每股收益（Earnings Per Share），ROI 和 RI。这些公司级别的会计指标与部门级别的会计指标存在很多相同的问题。因此，很多人认为应该使用市场指标来衡量公司的业绩。例如，股票回报率就被认为是一个重要的业绩衡量指标。

衡量公司的整体业绩和部门业绩是公司分配稀缺资源的一个重要考量。但，并不存在一个唯一的，最好的，最有效的业绩指标。此外，公司必须根据本身的地理位置，风俗习惯，经济条件和企业目标来制定适合自己的业绩指标。

章节概述：第九章
非财务业绩指标

本章的重点是非财务业绩指标，非财务业绩指标是财务业绩指标的补充而非替代。这些指标一般衡量公司和客户之间的关系，公司的经营状况，或公司的增长潜力。

通常我们认为非财务业绩指标预测了公司未来的长期表现，而财务业绩指标则反映了公司过去和暂时的业绩。前者被认为是超前指标而后者被认为是滞后指标。另一个关于非财务业绩指标的当前的观点是企业需要把它们的整体策略和非财务和财务指标挂钩。遵从这种观点，平衡计分卡提供了一种将企业的策略和财务以及非财务指标联系在一起的报表。

非财务业绩指标有产品质量，消费者满意度，生产力和市场份额。产品质量是产品或服务的整体可靠性。产品质量的一个很重要的方面是售出的产品中缺陷产品的比例。消费者满意度是衡量顾客对产品满意的程度。此项指标的重要指数有保修率和重复顾客的比例。生产力指的是生产效率或者说是产出投入比（例如每个工人每小时生产的产品数量）。最后，市场份额被很多世界知名公司视为一项重要的非财务指标。市场份额等于公司销售额除以整个行业的销售额。市场份额代表了顾客长期以来对公司的认同和因此带来的产品或服务额的增长。

在财务或非财务指标的使用上，并不存在一定的公式，能够完美的衡量公司业绩。关键是合理的结合两组指标。但找到正确的组合并不容易，因为存在无限种方式来组合这两组指标。

章节概述：第十章
转帐价格

本章向读者介绍转帐价格决策。转帐价格是同一公司各部门之间内部转移中间品时制定的价格。尽管销售中间品部门的收入就等于购买部门的费用，但公司的总利润还是有可能会受部门之间转帐价格的影响。原因是转帐价格可能会影响中间品的内部生产量和购买量。

转帐价格决策要遵循以下两个目标。第一，转帐价格应该鼓励部门的自主经营。第二，转帐价格应该保正部门目标和公司整体目标的一致。大多数情况下，很难制定一个同时符合以上两点的最优转帐价格。

本章讨论了三种制定转帐价格的方法。第一种方法是协议价格法。第二种是市场价格法。第三种是成本价格法。协议转帐价格由买方部门和卖方部门的协议决定，不受总部的干涉。在企业内部制定转帐价格，首先从外部市场的价格制定开始。假定存在中间品的外部市场，转帐价格的确立，应该起始于销售中间品部门在外部市场中销售此产品的价格或购买中间品部门在外部市场中购买此产品的价格。

当涉及利润分享时，很难通过协议制定转帐价格。例如，当处于优势地位的部门制定的价格对于另一个部门来说无法接受，那么产品的内部交换可能无法进行，因此公司作为整体会遭受损失。

市场价格法用外部市场价格来制定转帐价格。当中间品的市场是完全竞争的，市场价格法是最有效的。但当中间品市场是非完全竞争时，市场价格法就无效了。这种不完善通常会让内部销售部门制定一个比平均外部市场价格更高的价格，理由是一些难以量化的原因例如质量较高和运货时间较短。相反，购买部门会要求一个比市场价格低的价格。

成本转帐价格取决于中间品的生产成本。假如销售中间品的部门是利润中心或投资中心，转帐价格等于成本加设定利润。假如销售中间品的部门是成本中心，转帐价格等于交换部门的总成本。此方法也有几个不足之处。其中一个重要问题是销售部门可能没有动力去控制成本。因此，如果公司的目标是成本控制，成本转帐价格法下，部门目标会失去与公司目标的一致性。

企业所得税的差异对转帐价格也有影响。例如，提高转帐价格会将利润从购买部门转移到销售部门，而降低转帐价格则将利润从销售部门转移到购买部门。因此假如部门利润从高税率地区转移到低税率地区，公司税率总的来说在下降，而公司净利润则有所增加。因此，公司通常使用转帐价格来降低企业所得税。然而，大部分国家的税收法禁止通过转帐价格不合理转移利润。

章节概述：第十一章
营业预算和现金预算

预算是对公司未来业务的规划，通常（不是必须）以财务形式表现。大多数公司会做营业预算，长期投资预算和现金预算。本章的重点是营业预算和现金预算。比较实际数据和预算数据可以对企业进行控制。预算也可以用于规划，鼓励，协调和批准公司的业务。

营业预算规划部分的重点是预测下一期营业投入成本和产出收入。这些预测通常是过去经验和未来期望的组合。不同的预算方式对过去的业务有不同程度的反映。增量预算假定现期的营业水平在未来会继续保持某一水平。因此这种方法下，预算等于基数部分加上（减去）可能增加（减少）的部分。基数是预算中可能保持不变的部分。预算中增加的部分是由预算相关的业务变化引起的。增量预算的缺陷是基数部分通常包括了那些可能已经过时了的业务。

另一个可以解决增加预算缺陷的预算方法是零基预算。在零基预算的方法下，每年的预算都没有基数，整个预算用成本收益的准则来评估。此法增加了公司对环境变化的弹性和适应。然而，零基预算的方法非常耗费时间，它的成本也经常超过它的收益。因此，大部分企业会使用增量预算和零基预算的组合。

营业预算自然而然的给公司提供了对公司营业实施控制的机会。计算和分析实际财务结果和预算财务结果之间的差额可以帮助提高营业效率。预算差额也可以用来衡量经理人的业绩。假如经理层知道预算差额会被用来衡量他们的业绩，他们会努力就预算差额来提高业绩。当然，公司应对经理层进行控制并阻止任何不道德和非法行为来取得预算目标。

虽然 营业预算能激励雇员的表现，但很难估计雇员是受财务还是非财务动机的激励程度更大。预算在非财务方面对雇员的激励是对雇员企业共同目标的认同。当预算为参与性预算时，雇员会更努力实现预算目标。预算的非财务部分另一个激励雇员的方面是雇员实现个人目标的渴望。因此，普遍认为成功的预算应该设定有挑战性并且可完成的目标。

现金预算有利于公司管理当前和未来的现金需求。现金预算的主要目的是防止现金短缺或现金过量。现金预算有两步。第一步，期初的现金过量（或短缺）等于期初现金余额和本期所需现金之间的差额。第二步，估计后期的现金收入和现金支出。现金收入和支出涉及营业，投资和融资业务，这使得现金预算与营业预算和资本预算都有关联。

章节概述：第十二章
资本预算

资本费用（通常称作资本投资）是为了在多个营业周期中给公司带来收益。公司通常会做资本预算，资本预算是年度预计投资费用的清单。选择和控制投资费用的过程称做资本预算。

资本项目的选择分为两个阶段。第一，确定和公司总体目标相符合的投资项目。确定投资项目的方法之一是按项目类型分类，例如强制型，成本节约型和收入增加型。强制型项目是由外部带动，必需进行的投资。成本节约型项目与节约现有的经营成本的投资相关。收入增加型项目也是由外部带动的，与从新业务中增加收入或从现有业务中提高收入的投资相关。

一旦投资项目确定，资本预算过程的第二个阶段是每年实际选取要投资的项目。不同于资本确定阶段，资本选择阶段有一套正式的程序。资本选择阶段中使用的方法通常分为复杂型和简单型。复杂的方法会考虑与资本项目相关的风险，而简单项目则不会。净现值，利润指数和内部收益率是最常用的复杂型资本预算方法。最近几年，期权价格模型也被用于资本项目选择中。投资回收期和会计报酬率是最常用的简单型资本预算方法。

由于代理问题的存在（如第一章），经理层出于对短期业绩的考虑可能会不选择最优的投资项目。为了鼓励经理层作出对公司长期发展有利的决策，大部分企业采用了长期业绩评估机制。

资本预算的控制阶段经常被称为事后审计。事后审计是下一章的重点。

章节概述：第十三章
投资事后审计

本章的重点是资本预算过程的控制方面。资本投资（通常称资本项目）的控制涉及投资的事后审计。事后审计指的是对投资项目的评估和监控以确定是否投资达到了预期的目标。本章着重讨论事后审计的目的，过程和效果。

资本项目的事后审计有几个目的。首先，事后审计提供了一个财务控制机制。通过事后审计可以监控现金的流入和流出。第二，事后审计为未来资本费用提供投入并有助于公司利用以往经验改进未来的投资决策。第三，事后审计克服了与提出和结束项目相关的心理和政治问题。换句话，事后审计在一定程度上明确了经理层应付的责任。

事后审计的过程涉及实际结果和预期结果的比较，这种比较应与项目选择方式一致。而且，对事后审计过程的监管也需要考虑进去。实证研究表明精确的资本项目后期审计与公司业绩的提高密切相关。

许多公司面临对资本项目风险接受程度的问题。因为期望收益率和项目风险有直接的关系，公司如果不愿承担风险，就必须降低投资的期望收益率。事后审计可以帮助公司管理投资风险。有效的事后审计可以让公司确定哪些项目在投资过程中应该被改进或放弃。

不幸的是，资本预算的控制方面通常会被忽略。事后审计不仅帮助公司去掉不成功的项目，而且还可以帮助公司选择未来的投资项目。实证研究表明精确的事后审计可以提高公司的业绩，进而提高公司的价值。

章节概述：第十四章
企业改进的媒介－管理会计系统

企业能否生存部分取决于企业如何适应外部环境的变化。本章为管理会计系统作为企业对外部环境变化进行回应的媒介提出了一个概念框架。本框架强调了管理会计系统在便利企业发展方面的前瞻作用。此外，本框架还指明了企业结构和管理会计之间的联系。

管理会计系统应该并且已经成为促进企业发展的媒介，这点可由前面章节讨论的有关管理会计的以下两个领域说明。具体地说，管理会计中的业绩指标（例如剩余利润）和间接费用分摊（作业基础成本法）对管理会计系统如何推动企业发展提供了很好的例子。这些论点不仅有理论的基础，也已为大量的实证研究所验证。

MANAGERIAL ACCOUNTING:
CONCEPTS AND EMPIRICAL EVIDENCE
Sixth Edition

SOLUTIONS MANUAL

CHAPTER 1

Problem 1.1

Managerial accounting is the area of accounting concerned with the design and use of information systems that support managerial planning and control. Managerial economics, which is concerned with applying economic theory to managerial decision making (i.e., planning and control), can be thought of as the analytical (in terms of economic theory) arm of managerial economics. Decision support systems provide the computer-based environment (in terms of hardware and software) for carrying out managerial accounting and managerial economics.

Problem 1.2

Control is a process that consists of assessing whether the allocation of organizational resources has accomplished the desired objectives and, if not, determining the reallocation necessary to more closely attain those objectives. As such, effective control improves subsequent planning.

Problem 1.3

Strengths

- Explains why some accounting related concepts work well in some organizations, but not other organizations.

- Provides a framework for designing and implementing managerial accounting systems.

Weaknesses

- Difficult to understand all of the various relationships among contingency variables.

- Difficult to implement a contingency framework, even where the relationships are understood, in actual organizations.

Problem 1.4

1. Financial, ex post, internal (e.g., a firm's actual cost of producing a specific product);
2. Financial, ex post, external (e.g., a competitor's actual price for a specific product;
3. Financial, ex ante, internal (e.g., a firm's expected cost of producing a specific product);
4. Financial, ex ante, external (e.g., a competitor's expected price for a specific product);
5. Nonfinancial, ex post, internal (e.g., a firm's unit sales volume for a given product over the past year);
6. Nonfinancial, ex post, external (e.g., an industry's unit sales volume for a given product over the past year);
7. Nonfinancial, ex ante, internal (e.g., a firm's expected unit sales volume);
8. Nonfinancial, ex ante, external (e.g., an industry's expected unit sales volume).

Problem 1.5

Referring back to Figure 1.3, the decision tree would not include the High Cost (Low Cost) signal when in fact the Low Cost (High Cost) was the correct forthcoming result. In other words, the correct prediction would result with 100% accuracy. Thus, the expected payoff with a decision support cost system providing a perfect signal would be: $(.5) (1.0) (\$2,000,000 - \$1,000,000) = \$500,000$. Without the system the EV is $250,000. Hence, the maximum amount the firm should be willing to pay for the system is: $\$500,000 - \$250,000 = \$250,000$ (i.e., the firm's point of indifference).

Problem 1.6

A.   There are many issues that can be discussed here. Among them are the following:

1. access to vast financial databases
2. research (i.e., data mining capabilities)
3. the growth in electronic commerce
4. the Net facilitates managerial learning

B.   Ask students to look up a specific company (e.g., IBM) and to prepare
        an analysis of the company based on the data found in Edgar.

C.   www.irs.gov
        www.nyse.com
        www.bloomberg.com

Problem 1.7

A.   At least three reasons why an effective control system is necessary for
        JEM Associates, Inc., to realize their strategic goals for the next three
        years include:

   1.   Measurement of progress against established strategic control
        points ensuring goal congruence

   2.   Allowance for timely corrective action of identified problems

   3.   Adapting to changing conditions

B.   **Preliminary controls** are used to control input resources prior to the
        organizational transition process to prevent problems before they
        occur. Instead of waiting for results and comparing them with goals,
        control can be exerted by limiting activities in advance. These controls
        include policy manuals, budgets, rigid quality standards when
        purchasing from vendors, monitoring customer credit ratings before
        allowing purchases, and appropriate training programs for internal
        personnel.

        Screening controls are used to oversee the ongoing transformation
        process, guaranteeing that organizational objectives are being met.
        These controls are the heart of the control system. Included are quality
        controls while a product is being manufactured such as inspectors or
        calibration machines, and controls to ensure that a product is timely
        produced in the correct quantities. Also included are monitoring of
        labor productivity on a daily basis while the products are produced and
        online verification of customer accounts for the sales representatives.

        Post-action controls are used to control the output of the process after
        the transformation is completed and to provide corrective action for

problems encountered. These controls include variance analysis reports, analysis of scrapped material, performance evaluations, and feedback such as employee quality circles, customer surveys, and comments.

C.

1.   Employees frequently resist controls because controls may imply that someone else is watching or that the employee is now accountable to someone else. Controls can restrict the individual's actions that can negatively affect status and other social needs. Employees who naturally resist change may also resist controls due to a change in expertise and power structures and a lack of understanding or knowledge of organizational objectives.

2.   The characteristics that make controls effective and acceptable include:

- Employee participation in the establishment of valid performance standards in clear and concise terms (such as management by objectives) to increase employee acceptance.

- Timely feedback information with clear measurement and variance analysis.

- Checks and balances within the system to ensure objective evaluation of employee performance that includes positive reinforcement and rewards.

Problem 1.8

A.   A description of the characteristics of three other operational support systems and an example of each is presented below.

1.   Real-time systems process data from on-going operations almost immediately as the data are entered into the computer. Data are analyzed and processed with the databases being

updated and making current information available while the operations are in progress.

Typical features of real-time accounting applications include:

- On-line input and processing of information that uses direct-access files so that data stored within a computer system can be retrieved directly and immediately from on-line storage.

- Time-sharing so that different users can obtain information simultaneously from the computer system.

An example of a real-time system is an airline reservations system.

2.   Interactive systems are real-time systems that allow users to converse or dialogue with a computer. This enables users to answer processing questions or provide additional data or instructions.

An example of an interactive system is a production and inventory control system.

3.   Communication-based systems are systems whose functions are to receive inquiries or transaction data from individuals at remote locations, to transmit the received inputs to a central computer location for processing, and to re-transmit the processed information back to remote locations for decision-making purposes.

An example of a communication-based system is a network of minicomputers located at various locations of a retail chain that transmit data to the central mainframe.

B.

1.   The purpose of a decision support system (DSS) is to improve the efficiency and effectiveness of managerial decisions in the areas of planning and forecasting.

The characteristics and capabilities of decision support systems (DSS) include:

- The handling of unstructured problems and non-routine data. DSS are aimed at relatively unstructured problems (i.e., problems with no clear solution procedures and, therefore, require managerial judgement).

- Simulation. Probabilities and expectations are used to simulate a particular situation.

2. Expert systems are artificial intelligence software packages that use facts, knowledge, and reasoning techniques to solve problems that typically require human expert abilities. The purposes of expert systems are varied, including assisting in learning, helping to train decision makers, and even making decisions.

The characteristics and capabilities of expert systems include:

- Tracing logic. Most expert systems must be able to retrace the logic they followed to reach a conclusion, and usually are also required to communicate this to users on display screens or printed output. Thus, at any given point during a session, a user is able to input an answer to a question, ask the system why it is asking the question, and at the end, ask how a conclusion was reached.

- Certainty factors. The data input to most operational systems (and some decision support systems) are known with certainty and, therefore, treated as constants. In contrast, expert systems allow users to assign probability factors to data (i.e., a given situation or event is likely to occur a specified percentage of the time).

Problem 1.9

A. Expected value without cost-predicting system
    = 60% × ($4,000,000 – $5,000,000) + 40% × ($4,000,000 –
    $1,000,000)
    = $600,000

    Expected value (EV) with cost-predicting system

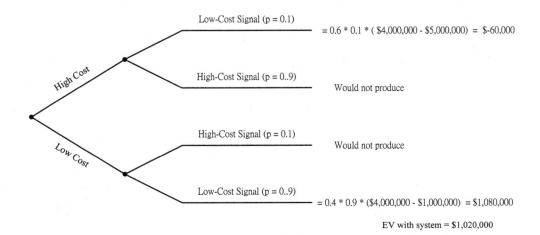

Low-Cost Signal (p = 0.1)
= 0.6 * 0.1 * ($4,000,000 - $5,000,000) = $-60,000

High-Cost Signal (p = 0..9)
Would not produce

High-Cost Signal (p = 0.1)
Would not produce

Low-Cost Signal (p = 0..9)
= 0.4 * 0.9 * ($4,000,000 - $1,000,000) = $1,080,000

EV with system = $1,020,000

    Therefore, expected value with cost-predicting system
    = $ 1,080,000 + $(-60,000) – $600,000 = $420,000 < $600,000

    Since the expected value with the cost-predicting system is less than
    that without the cost-predicting system, the company should produce
    and sell the new pocket PC without the purchase of the cost-predicting
    system.

B. If the cost-predicting system provided perfect information, the
    expected value would be $1,200,000 (i.e., [0.41 x [$4,000,000 -
    $1,000,000]).

    $1,200,000 - $600,000 (cost of the system) = $600,000

Thus, with perfect information the net expected value of this project would be exactly the same with or without the cost-predicting system. Accordingly, your decision probably would not change (i.e., you would go ahead with the project without the cost-predicting system).

CHAPTER 2

Problem 2.1

		Old	New
A.	Contribution Margin (P-VC)	$4	$6
	Fixed Costs	$1,600	$2,700

$$\pi = 4X - 1,600 = 6X - 2,700 - 400$$
$$4X - 1,600 = 6X - 3,100$$
$$2X = 1,500$$
$$X = 750$$

$$\pi = \$1,400 \text{ (Old)} / \$1,800 \text{ (New)}$$

The firm expects to sell 750 units. Using the old equipment, this will result in profits of $1400. However, if the firm switches to using the new equipment, profits increase to $1800. Thus, the switch to new equipment will result in a $400 increase in profits.

B. $\pi = 4X - 1,600 = 6X - 2,700$
$$2X = 1,100$$
$$X = 550$$

Check on Solution	Old	New
Sales = 550 units		
Total Contribution	$2,200	$3,300
Less: Fixed Costs	- 1,600	- 2,700
Profits	$ 600	$ 600

C.   Old BE = $\dfrac{\$1,600}{\$4}$ = 400 units

New BE = $\dfrac{\$2,700}{\$6}$ = 450 units

At 550 units profits are $600 under either option.

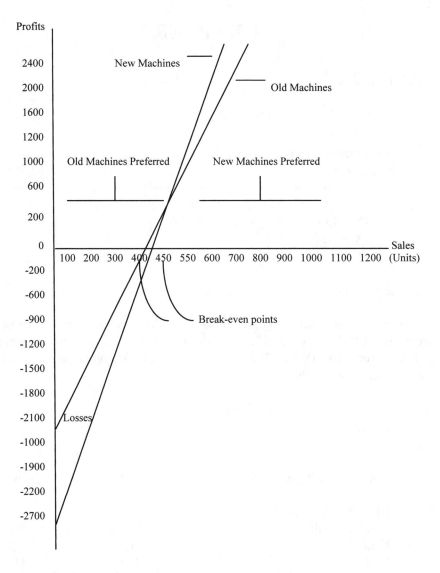

D. At a sales level of 550 units per month, the firm is indifferent between the two options. At sales levels below 550 units, the old system is preferred because the leverage from the larger fixed costs only becomes profitable after the 550 point of indifference. At sales levels above 550 units per month, the new equipment option is more profitable (i.e., the leverage from the new equipment pays off).

Problem 2.2

1. Contribution Margin (P-VC): $2,000 – ($450+$250) = $1,300 per laptop
2. $X_{BE} = FC/(P-VC) = \$5000,000/\$1,300 = 385$ laptops per year
3. $X\pi = (FC+\pi)/(P-VC) = [\$500,000 + \$1,000,000]/\$1,300 = 1,154$ laptops per year

Problem 2.3

Sales price less direct and variable costs x number of units sold = contribution margin
($100 – ($30 + $20 + $10 + $12)) x 900 units = $25,200. The answer is b.

Problem 2.4

The answer is b.

Problem 2.5

A.   BE units = $\dfrac{\text{Total Fixed Costs}}{\text{Weighted Average CM Per Basket}}$

Weighted average CM = (2,000 x 1) + (800 x 5) + (300 x 10) = 9,000

Total Fixed Costs = 1,200,000 + 2,000,000 + 3,000,000 + 1,000,000 = 7,200,000

BE Baskets = $\dfrac{7,200,000}{9,000}$ = 800 Baskets

- State of the art = 800 x 1 = 800 units

- Professional = 800 x 5 = 4,000 units

- Standard = 800 x 10 = 8,000 units

B. Profit From Products Before Reduction of Price

State (2,000 x 1,000) – 1,200,000 = $ 800,000

Professional (800 x 5,000) – 2,000,000 =   2,000,000

Standard (300 x 10,000) – 3,000,000 =   _____0____

Sub-Total   2,800,000
    Less Joint Fixed Costs   1,000,000
                                                        $1,800,000

After Price Reduction

State (1,500 x 2,000) – 1,200,000 = $1,800,000

Professional (800 x 4,500) – 2,000,000 =   1,600,000

Standard (300 x 9,000) – 3,000,000 =   - 300,000

Sub-Total   3,100,000
    Less Joint Fixed Costs   1,000,000
                                                        $2,100,000

Conclusion: Go for it, since there is an increase in profit of $300,000.

C. Effect of Increase in Advertising Expenditure

State (2,000 x 1,500) – 1,200,000 = $1,800,000

Professional (800 x 7,000) – 2,000,000 =   3,600,000

Standard (300 x 13,000) – 3,000,000 =   ___900,000

Sub-Total   6,300,000
    Less Joint Fixed Costs (5,000,000 + 1,000,000)   6,000,000

Profit $ 300,000

Conclusion: Since the profit decreases from $1,800,000 to $300,000, the advertising campaign should not be undertaken.

Problem 2.6

A.
$$
\begin{array}{ll}
P = & \$15,000 \\
VC = & \underline{5,000} \\
CM = & \underline{\$10,000}
\end{array}
$$

$$
\begin{array}{lr}
\text{Fixed Costs (Other Than Salaries)} = & \$\ 80,000 \\
\text{Fixed Salaries} & \underline{80,000} \\
& \underline{\$160,000}
\end{array}
$$

$$
BE_x = \frac{\$160,000}{\$10,000} = 16 \text{ clients}
$$

B.
$$
BE_x = \frac{\$80,000 + \$80,000/(1 - .2)}{\$10,000} = 18 \text{ clients}
$$

C. Fixed Costs = $80,000 + $120,000 = $200,000

$$
X = \frac{\$200,000}{\$10,000} = 20 \text{ clients}
$$

D. (1) Based on $40,000 salary: Total Fixed Costs = $160,000 - $48,000 = $112,000

$$
\begin{array}{ll}
P = & \$15,000 \\
\text{New VC} = & \underline{7,000} \\
\text{New MC} = & \underline{\$\ 8,000}
\end{array}
$$

$$
BE_x = \frac{\$112,000}{\$8,000} = 14 \text{ (clients)} < 16
$$

(2) Based on $60,000 salary: Total Fixed Costs = $200,000 - $48,000
= $152,000

$$BE_x = \frac{\$152,000}{\$8,000} = 19 \text{ (clients)} < 20$$

On balance, the trade-off seems favorable in this problem.

Problem 2.7

A)   Both companies have total operating costs = $40,000
   (Alpha: $20,000 + $20,000)
   (Beta: $30,000 + $10,000)

   Fixed costs to total operating costs ratio
   Alpha: $20,000 / $40,000 = 50%
   Beta: $10,000 / $40,000 = 25%
   Therefore, Alpha Co. has higher operating leverage

B)

	Alpha Co.	Beta Co.
Sales	$100,000	$100,000
Total Variable Costs	40,000	60,000
Contribution Margin	60,000	40,000
Fixed Costs	20,000	10,000
Profits	$40,000	30,000
Profit (per unit)	$40	30

The reason why the profit per unit changes is that fixed cost does not change with change in the sales quantity. Since Alpha Co. has a higher operating leverage than Beta Co., its profit per unit increased 100% whereas the profit per unit only went up by 50% for Beta Co.

Problem 2.8

A.   (3)
B.   (2)
C.   (1)
D.   (3)

Problem 2.9

A.

1. To earn the projected net income of $1,800,000, Kipmar Company needs to sell $50,000,000 of its molded briefcase, calculated as follows:

    Calculation of contribution margin ratio.

	Current	Projected
Selling price	$40.00	$40.00
Variable costs		
Direct material	12.00	13.80
Direct labor	5.80	5.80
Variable overhead	4.80	4.80
Selling expenses	3.00	3.00
Total variable costs	25.60	27.40
Contribution margin	$14.40	$12.60
Contribution margin ratio	36.0% [1]	31.5% [1]

    [1] Contribution margin ratio = Contribution margin ÷ selling price

    Calculation of the gross profit needed to earn the projected net income of $1,800,000.

    Gross profit = net profit ÷ (1 – income tax rate) = $1,800,000 ÷(1 - .4) = $3,000,000

    Calculation of the gross sales needed to earn a gross profit of $3,000,000.

    Gross sales = (gross profit + fixed costs) ÷ contribution margin ratio = [$3,000,000 + ($7,800,000 + $1,550,000 + $3,250,000 + $150,000)] ÷ .315 = $15,750,000 ÷ .315 = $50,000,000

2. Kipmar Company would have to charge $42.81 for the molded briefcase in order to maintain the same contribution ratio of 36.0 percent, calculated as follows:

63

Selling price = projected unit variable cost ÷ (1 − current contribution margin ratio = $27.40 ÷ (1 - .36) = $42.81

B.   Kipmar Company would need to sell 500,000 units of the molded briefcase and 125,000 units of the leather briefcase as calculated below.

	Molded Briefcase	Leather Briefcase
Selling price	$40.00	$90.00
Variable costs		
Direct material	13.80	18.50
Direct labor	5.80	7.50
Variable overhead	4.80	6.00
Selling expenses	3.00	4.00
Total variable costs	27.40	36.00
Contribution margin	$12.60	$54.00
Mix 4:1	.80	.20
Weighted unit contribution	$10.08 [1]	$10.80 [1]

[1] Total weighted unit contribution = $10.08 + $10.80 = $20.88

Break-even in unit volume	= Fixed costs + weighted unit contribution
	= ($12,750,000 + $300,000) ÷ $20.88
	= $13,050,000 ÷ $20.88 = 625,000 units
Molded briefcase	= 625,000 x .8 = 500,000 units
Leather briefcase	= 625,000 x .2 = 125,000 units

Problem 2.10

	Firm A	Firm B
Break-even*	$3,750,000	$4,000,000
Fixed Costs*	1,500,000	2,000,000
Π *	900,000	1,000,000
* Given		
Contribution Margin %	$\dfrac{1,500,000}{3,750,000} = 40\%$	$\dfrac{2,000,000}{4,000,000} = 50\%$
VC/Sales	60%	50%
Current Sales (S)	900,000 = S (.4) – 1,500,000 S = $6,000,000	1,000,000 = S (.5) – 2,000,000 S = $6,000,000

A.

Profits are equal at: $.4S - \$1,500,000 = .5S - \$2,000,000$, therefore, $S = \$5,000,000$; where $\Pi = \$500,000$; $\$6,000,000 - \$5,000,000 = \$1,000,000$ (see work above).

B.

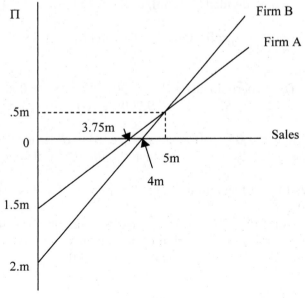

Problem 2.11

A.

    1.   A total of 480 seminar participants is needed for the joint venture to break even. Calculated as follows:

             The break-even number of participants equals the fixed costs divided by the contribution margin per participant.

             Fixed costs (FC = $318,000 from GSI + $210,000 from Eastern = $528,000

             Contribution margin (CM) = $1,200 fee – ($47 + $18 + $35) variable costs = $1,100

             Break-even = FC/CM = $528,000/$1,100 = <u>480</u> seminar participants

    2.   A total of 700 seminar participants is needed for the joint venture to earn a net income of $169,000 calculated as follows:

             The target number of participants equals the fixed costs plus the desired operating profit, divided by the contribution margin per participant. The desired operating profit equals the net income divided by (1 minus the tax rate).

             Operating profit (OP) = $169,000/(1 - .30) = $169,000/.70 = $242,000

             Target participants = (FC + OP)/CM = ($528,000 + $242,000)/$1,100 = $770,000/$1,100 = <u>700</u> participants

B.   A minimum of 1,055 participants is needed in order for GSI to prefer the 40 percent fee option rather than the flat fee. Calculated as follows:

GSI fees for flat fee option = $9,500 per seminar x 40 seminars = $380,000
GSI fees for 40% of Eastern's profit-before-tax option = 40% [(contribution margin x number of participants) – fixed cost] = .40 x [($1,100 x N) - $210,000] = $440 x N - $84,000.

GSI fees are equal for the two options at the following number of participants:

$380,000 = $440 x N - $84,000
$464,000 = $440 x N
$464,000/$440 = N = <u>1,054.5</u> participants

Therefore, GSI will earn more revenue and prefer the 40 percent option when the number of participants is 1,055 or higher.

CHAPTER 3

Problem 3.1

A job costing system is most appropriate for custom made products, where products vary from customer to customer. A process costing system is most appropriate for mass produced products, where no distinction exists between the product being purchased by one customer versus another customer. A hybrid costing system (i.e., something between job order and process costing) is particularly useful when some manufacturing costs (e.g., conversion costs) are similar, but other costs (e.g., direct materials) vary across products.

Problem 3.2

The answer is b.

Problem 3.3

The answer is c.

Problem 3.4

A.   Direct Materials

Beginning	$10,000
+Purchase	22,000
	32,000
-Ending	15,000

Direct materials put into production	$17,000
Direct labor	30,000
O/H (@ 50% of DL	15,000
Total mfg. costs	$62,000

W/P:
+beginning $40,000
- ending   18,000   22,000
F/G
+ beginning   30,000
- ending   **60,000** *   30,000
C/S 60% of $9,000 sales $54,000

    *   F/G at time of fire was $60,000

B.   No. The numbers provided in the problem provide a snapshot at a moment in time. Accordingly, the answer to this problem would be the same under a process costing system, providing the numbers given in the problem were the correct ones to use.

Some students will correctly argue that the numbers would almost certainly be different under the two costing systems. However, the problem essentially asks what the answer would be if the numbers in the problem applied to a process costing system, rather than a job order costing system.

Problem 3.5

Product cost data is important information for various decisions including: production level decisions, inventory level decisions, pricing decisions, and new product decisions. Unfortunately, determining the cost of a product is as much an art as it is a science. Thus, a manager who does not understand how such costs are derived loses much flexibility in making the above type decisions.

Problem 3.6

Costs of having a JIT system include:

1.   Increased dependency on suppliers
2.   Unexpected increased demand is difficult to handle
3.   Economies of scale may not be achieved
4.   Temporary shutdown in one department can have large ripple effects

Costs of not having a JIT system include:

1. Storage costs
2. Financing charges
3. Obsolete inventory
4. Increased throughput time

Problem 3.7

Question Number 4 (A2/3/4)

A. A job order cost system is appropriate in any environment where costs can be readily identified with specific products, batches, contracts, or projects.

B. The only job remaining in ErgoFurn, Inc.'s work-in-process inventory at May 31, 2003, is Job PS812. The dollar value of Job PS812 can be calculated as follows:

Job PS812 balance 4/30/03		$250,000
May additions:		
Raw material	$124,000	
Purchased parts	87,000	
Labor costs	200,500	
Factory overhead 19,500 hours x $5.00 [(1)]	97,500	509,000
Work-in-process inventory 5/31/03		$759,000

[(1)] Factory overhead rate = $\dfrac{\$4,500,000}{900,000 \ hours}$ = $5.00 per hour

C. The dollar value of the chairs remaining in ErgoFurn, Inc.'s finished goods inventory at May 31, 2003, is $455,600, calculated as follows:

Calculation of units of chairs in finished goods inventory at May 31, 2003.

	Chair Units
Finished goods inventory, 4/30/03	19,400
Units completed in May	15,000
Units available	34,400
Less: Units shipped in May	21,000
Finished goods inventory, 5/31/03	13,400

Since ErgoFurn uses the first-in, first-out (FIFO) inventory method, all units remaining in finished goods inventory were completed in May.

Unit cost of chairs completed in May.

Work-in-process inventory, 4/30/03		$431,000
May additions:		
Raw materials	$ 3,000	
Purchased parts	10,800	
Labor costs	43,200	
Factory overhead (4,400 x $5.00)	22,000	79,000
Total cost		$510,000

$$\text{Unit cost} = \frac{Total\ cost}{Units\ completed} = \frac{\$510,000}{15,000} = \underline{\$\ 34}\ \text{per unit}$$

Value of finished goods inventory = unit cost x quantity = $34 x 13,400 = $455,600

D.   If the amount of overapplied or underapplied overhead is not material, or the result of an error in the overhead application rate, the amount is generally treated as a period cost and charged to cost of goods sold. If the amount is significant, the amount should be prorated over the relevant accounts, i.e., work-in-process inventory, finished goods inventory, and cost of goods sold.

Problem 3.8

A.

    1.   The equivalent units for each cost element, using the weighted average method, are presented below.

	Direct Materials		Conversion
	Chemicals	Cans	
Units completed & transferred to shipping	20,000	20,000	20,000
Work-in-process at 5/31			
Chemicals (100%)	5,000		
Cans (0%)		0	
Conversion costs (80%)			4,000
Equivalent units	25,000	20,000	24,000

    2.   The equivalent units for each cost element, using the first-in, first-out method, are presented below.

	Direct Materials		Conversion
	Chemicals	Cans	
Transferred to shipping from 5/1 work-in-process (4,000 @ 25%)			
Chemicals (0%)	0		
Cans (100%)		4,000	
Conversion costs (75%)			3,000
Current production transferred to shipping (100%)	16,000	16,000	16,000
5/31 work-in-process (5,000 @80%)			
Chemicals (100%)	5,000		
Cans (0%)		0	
Conversion costs (80%)			4,000
Equivalent units	21,000	20,000	23,000

B.

    1.   The cost per equivalent unit for each cost element, using the weighted average method, is presented below.

	Direct Materials		Conversion*
	Chemicals	Cans	
Work-in-process at 5/1	$ 45,600	$ 0	$ 8,125
May costs added	228,400	7,000	45,500
Total costs	$274,000	$ 7,000	$53,625
÷	÷	÷	÷
Weighted average equivalent units	25,000	20,000	24,000
Cost per equivalent units	$ 10.96	$ .35	$ 2.23

*Conversion cost = direct labor + factory overhead

    2.   The cost per equivalent unit for each cost element, using the first-in, first-out method, is presented below.

	Direct Materials		Conversion
	Chemicals	Cans	
May costs incurred	$228,400	$ 7,000	$45,500
÷			
First-in, first-out equivalent units	21,000	20,000	23,000
Cost per equivalent units	$ 10.88	$ .35	$ 1.98

Problem 3.9

A. Byrd Company's operating income for 2002 and 2003, using absorption costing, is $54,500 and $54,300, respectively, as calculated in Exhibit 1 below.

<table>
<tr><td colspan="3">EXHIBIT 1</td></tr>
<tr><td colspan="3">Operating Income Under Absorption Costing</td></tr>
<tr><td></td><td>2002</td><td>2003</td></tr>
<tr><td>Sales [1]</td><td>$150,000</td><td>$170,000</td></tr>
<tr><td>Beginning inventory [2]</td><td>54,000</td><td>84,000</td></tr>
<tr><td>Cost of goods manufactured [3]</td><td>120,000</td><td>24,000</td></tr>
<tr><td>Cost of goods available</td><td>174,000</td><td>108,000</td></tr>
<tr><td>Less: Ending inventory [4]</td><td>84,000</td><td>6,000</td></tr>
<tr><td>Cost of goods sold at standard cost</td><td>90,000</td><td>102,000</td></tr>
<tr><td>Net unfavorable variance</td><td>1,000</td><td>1,000</td></tr>
<tr><td>Production volume variance</td><td>---</td><td>8,000</td></tr>
<tr><td>Adjusted cost of goods sold</td><td>91,000</td><td>111,000</td></tr>
<tr><td>Gross margin</td><td>59,000</td><td>59,000</td></tr>
<tr><td>Variable marketing & administrative costs [6]</td><td>1,500</td><td>1,700</td></tr>
<tr><td>Fixed marketing & administrative costs</td><td>3,000</td><td>3,000</td></tr>
<tr><td>Operating income</td><td>$ 54,500</td><td>$ 54,300</td></tr>
</table>

Notes:

	2002	**2003**
[1]	1,500 units x $100	1,700 units x $100
[2]	900 units x $60*	1,400 units x $60

* Unit cost is comprised of prime cost + variable overhead + fixed overhead:
   $40 + $15 + $5** = $60 per unit
**Fixed overhead per unit: $10,000 ÷ 2,000 units = $5 per unit

| [3] | 2,000 units x $60 | 400 units x $60 |
| [4] | 1,400* units x $60 | 100* units x $60 |

* Ending inventory, in units, is comprised of beginning inventory + production sales
   900 + 2,000 – 1,500 = 1,400 units   1,400 + 400 – 1,700 = 100 units

| [5] | --- | 1,600* units x $5 |

* Unit production variance, in units, is comprised of normal activity – actual production

| | --- | 2,000 – 400 = 1,600 units |
| [6] | 1,500 units x $1 | 1,700 units x $1 |

74

B.   Byrd Company's operating income for 2002 and 2003, using variable costing, is $52,000 and $60,800, respectively, as calculated in Exhibit 2 below.

EXHIBIT 2
Operating Income Under Variable Costing

	2002	2003
Sales [1]	$150,000	$170,000
Cost of good sold		
Beginning inventory [2]	49,500	77,000
Cost of goods manufactured [3]	110,000	22,000
Cost of goods available	159,500	99,000
Less: Ending inventory [4]	77,000	5,500
Cost of goods sold at standard cost	82,500	93,500
Net unfavorable variance	1,000	1,000
Adjusted cost of goods sold	83,500	94,500
Variable marketing & administrative costs [5]	1,500	1,700
Total variable costs	85,000	96,200
Contribution margin	65,000	73,800
Fixed marketing & administrative costs	3,000	3,000
Fixed manufacturing overhead	10,000	10,000
Operating income	$ 52,000	$ 60,800

Notes:

2002	2003
[1] 1,500 units x $100	1,700 units x $100
[2] 900 units x $55*	1,400 units x $55

* Unit cost is comprised of prime cost + variable overhead: $40 + $15 - $55 per unit

2002	2003
[3] 2,000 units x $55	400 units x $55
[4] 1,400 units x $55	100 units x $55
[5] 1,500 units x $1	1,700 units x $1

CHAPTER 4

Problem 4.1

Strengths

- Facilitates planning and control
- It averages out aberrations in various production costs due to periodic increases (decreases) in input prices and/or activity levels
- In situations where the compilation of actual costs lags behind the production of goods, it permits timely product costs

Weaknesses

- Assumes costs are relatively stable
- It averages costs over a large number of units rather than computing the actual costs of particular units (i.e., this is both a strength and weakness)

Problem 4.2

The planning and control aspects of standard costing provides a mechanism by which firms can conduct cost management on both an ex ante and ex post basis. For example, a standard costing system can help a firm assess whether expected costs, and related pricing decisions, are competitive for the product(s) under consideration. The control (i.e., ex post) aspect of a standard costing system can help a firm improve its future operations, which also provides a tool for global competitiveness.

Problem 4.3

A. Since volume variances are a function of production, rather than sales, the charging of such variances to cost of goods sold results (to a limited extent) in the situation described by the Controller.

B.   If units produced are never sold, such profits are never realized. Alternatively, if the units produced are sold in the distant future, the present value of the future sales needs to be determined to derive the appropriate profits.

C.   No. In this case, volume variances would be proportionally divided among units sold, units in finished goods, and work-in-process inventories.

D.   Standard cost variances are usually insignificant relative to total cost of goods sold. Hence, the situation described by the Controller usually does not have any practical implication.

Problem 4.4

The primary purpose of a standard costing system is to facilitate planning and control. Standard cost systems are especially useful where products (including services) and/or activities lend themselves to some sort of standardized routine. Many services offered by a hospital lend themselves to a set of activities which can be standardized. For these services, a standard costing system should help facilitate planning and control, and in turn cost efficiency. Indeed, the basic premise underlying much of the health care revolution is to foster a more cost efficient health maintenance program via a form of standard costing. (Of course, to the extent a standard costing system is being forced upon services that do not lend themselves to being standardized, the ultimate quality of the service may be compromised.)

Problem 4.5

(Standard price – actual price) x number of pounds purchased
($0.72 - $0.75) x 4,500 pounds = $135 unfavorable
The answer is c.

Problem 4.6

A. Since there were no inventories at the beginning of the first quarter or at the end of the second quarter, total materials purchased in the two quarters combined should equal the total materials used in the two quarters combined. Given that all the materials were purchased in the first quarter:

- Pounds of material purchased in the first quarter = Pounds of material used in the two quarters for production

- Pounds of material used in the two quarters for production = Standard material usage + Excess material usage

  $\qquad$ = [Standard cost of materials/Standard cost per pound] + [Material usage variance/Standard cost per pound]
  $\qquad$ = [(600,000 + 540,000)/60] + [(-30,000 + 54,000)/60]
  $\qquad$ = 19,000 + 400
  $\qquad$ = 19,400

B. Actual price per pound = Standard price per pound ± Material price variance per pound
  $\qquad$ = 60 ± [Total material price variance/Pounds of material purchased]
  $\qquad$ = 60 +* [194,000/19,400**]
  $\qquad$ = 60 + 10
  $\qquad$ = $70

  * Since the material price variance is unfavorable, the actual price is higher than the standard price of the material. Hence, the material price variance per pound is added, not subtracted.
  **From A. above.

C. The business manager has not manipulated the income statement in the second quarter to report an increase in net income despite the fall in sales. The results obtained here are peculiar to firms that isolate price variance at the time of purchase rather than at the time of usage: the fact that all materials were purchased in the first quarter has exacerbated the problem further. The income statement would have reported a net income of $185,000 and $67,000 for the first and second quarters respectively, if the firm had isolated the material price variance at the time of usage instead of isolating them at the time of purchase (see the income statement below).

INCOME STATEMENT FOR THE FIRST TWO QUARTERS (Assuming Material Price Variances are Isolated at the Time of Usage		
	I Quarter	**II Quarter**
Standard gross profit (as before, see Exhibit A of the problem)	$300,000	$270,000
Material price variance	95,000 U	99,000 U
Material usage variance	30,000 F	54,000 U
General and administrative costs	50,000	50,000
Net income	$185,000	$ 67,000

Problem 4.7

A.   For Leather Works, the variances for the month of May 2005 are calculated as follows:

- Material price variance
  (Standard price – actual price) x actual materials used
  ($7.50 - $8.10) x 8,500 feet = $5,100 unfavorable

  The actual price is calculated by dividing actual material costs ($68,850) by actual feet of material used (8,500).

- Material efficiency variance
  (Standard material usage – act usage) x standard price
  (8,700 – 8,500) x $7.50 = $1,500 favorable

  The standard usage is calculated by multiplying the standard feet per unit by the number of units (3 feet x 2,900 units).

- Labor rate variance
  (Standard rate – actual rate) x actual hours worked
  ($14.00 - $14.10) x 1,837.6 hours = $183.76 unfavorable

  The actual labor rate is calculated by dividing actual labor costs by actual hours worked (25,910 / 1,837.6 hours).

- Labor efficiency variance
  (Standard time worked – actual time) x standard rate
  (2,175 hours – 1,837.6 hours) x $14 per hour = $4,723.60
  favorable

  The standard time is calculated by multiplying the standard time per unit by the total units made and expressed in hours (45 minutes / 60 minutes per hour) x 2,900 units.

B.   The six-month trend shows that the material price variance remains unfavorable, but is improving; the material efficiency variance remains favorable, but is decreasing; the labor rate variance is stable and insignificant; and the labor efficiency variance remains favorable, but is decreasing. Since this is a union shop, the company should not expect to observe significant labor rate variances. The other three variances are problematic, however. Ideally, variances should behave in the manner of a statistical control chart. That is, the variances should appear to be random unless the process itself has been changed. The trends noted above indicate that the standards have not been set properly and are ineffective as a control technique.

Problem 4.8

A.   While the costs and activity were planned to be evenly distributed throughout the year, Smylan's actual activity was less than estimated. Thus, the actual variable manufacturing costs should be compared to a flexible budget set at the actual activity levels.

B.   A detailed variance analysis of manufacturing overhead for Smylan Company for the current month is presented below.

	Applied Overhead	Budget at Standard Machine Hours Allowed (8,000)	Budget at Actual Machine Hours (8,050)	Actual Costs
Variable	$ 96,000(1)	$ 96,000(1)	$ 96,600(2)	$ 95,800
Fixed	176,000	220,000(4)	220,000(4)	211,200
	$272,000(3)	$316,000	$316,600	$307,000

Total variance $35,000 U

(1)   8,000 x $12
(2)   8,050 x $12
(3)   8,000 x $34
(4)   2,640,000 / 12

1.   Variable overhead spending variance
        Actual machine hours (8,050) x standard cost $96,600
        Actual variable overhead   95,800 $800F

2.   Variable overhead efficiency variance
        Budget at standard machine hours (8,000)   96,000
        Actual machine hours (8,050) x standard costs   96,600   600U

3.   Fixed overhead budget / spending variance
        Budget ($2,640,000 / 12 months)   220,000
        Actual   211,200   8,800F

4.   Fixed overhead volume variance
        Applied (8,000 x $22) (i.e., std. F/o for
            Prod. Achieved   176,000
        Budget   220,000   44,000U

C.

    1.   The fixed overhead volume variance (sometimes referred to as the fixed overhead denominator variance) measures how well a company uses its fixed manufacturing capacity as measured by the activity base selected.

    2.   Frank Paige can eliminate the fixed overhead volume variance by increasing Smylan Company's production up to the expected activity level for the month.

    3.   Increasing production would not necessarily be in the best interest of Frank Paige and Smylan Company. The only way to reduce the fixed overhead volume variance would be to increase production and produce more units, which would increase Smylan's inventory of furnished goods at a time of reduced demand. This would result in an increased investment in inventory plus additional inventory storage costs.

CHAPTER 5

Problem 5.1

A.   True
B.   False
C.   True
D.   True
E.   False
F.   True
G.   False

Problem 5.2

Even where a firm produces only one product via one activity, it is necessary to allocate certain costs to different time periods. In organizations which produce more than one product and engage in several activities, the allocation of costs among products and activities is a fundamental issue. Further, keeping in mind that a given cost can be related to more than one cost objective, the decisions related to various products, activities, and subunits are all affected by the way costs are allocated.

Problem 5.3

A.   Yes. Given that a large percentage of costs within a university are indirect with respect to the key cost objectives of measuring the costs of producing well-educated students and the costs of running a department within the university, charging a 35% overhead rate for such grants may well be a reasonable approach.

B.   If the goal of a university were to maximize the dollar amount of external research grants, at least two related issues need to be considered. First, it is necessary to determine the penalties associated with research grants that actually lose money. Second, a distinction needs to be made between grants which are awarded on a cost basis and those awarded on a low-bid basis.

If research grants are not required to cover all of their costs (i.e., the university is prepared to subsidize such grants), the 35% overhead rate may unnecessarily impede the success rate of having proposals funded. Alternatively, if each research grant is intended to recover all of its costs, then a separation between fixed and variable costs becomes a significant issue (at least in the short-run). In the latter case, a flat rate of 35% may unduly affect the acceptance of some proposals and the rejection of other proposals. Of course, the degree to which these factors ultimately affect grant proposal success will be influenced by the degree of competition for specific grant money. Where grants are awarded on a low-bid basis (e.g., on a quasi university research-industry proposal), these concerns become accelerated.

C.   No. Maximizing the dollar amount of external research grants is not synonymous with maximizing the quality of research output, let alone the idea of maximizing the output of well-educated students.

Problem 5.4

Regression analysis is a good way to statistically assess the relationship between a dependent variable and one of more independent variables. Since the allocation of indirect costs requires the identification of those factors which drive such costs, regression analysis provides a useful statistical technique for accomplishing this objective (i.e., the indirect costs can be thought of as the dependent variable and the cost drivers as the independent variables).

Problem 5.5

The answer for A is a. The answer for B is b.

Problem 5.6

A.

> 1. & 2. Using computer usage time as the application base for the Information Systems Department and square feet of floor space for the Facilities Department, the application of overhead from

the service departments under the Direct and Step Methods, are presented below.

Direct Method

	Service Departments		Production Departments		
	IS	Facilities	Programming	Consulting	Training
Budgeted overhead	$50,000	$25,000	$ 75,000	$110,000	$ 85,000
Proportion of service furnished:					
By IS: (1)			12/27	6/27	9/27
Allocation	($50,000)		$ 22,222	$ 11,111	$ 16,667
By Facilities: (2)			4/18	6/18	8/18
Allocation		($25,000)	$ 5,556	$ 8,333	$ 11,111
Totals			$102,778	$129,444	$112,778

(1) Allocated on the basis of 2,700 hours of computer usage.

(2) Allocated on the basis of 1,800 thousand square feet of floor space.

Step Method

	IS	Facilities	Programming	Consulting	Training
Budgeted overhead	$50,000	$ 25,000	$ 75,000	$110,000	$ 85,000
Proportion of service furnished:					
By IS: (1)		3/30	12/30	6/30	9/30
Allocation	($50,000)	$ 5,000	$ 20,000	$ 10,000	$ 15,000
By Facilities: (2)			4/18	6/18	8/18
Allocation		($30,000)	$ 6,667	$ 10,000	$ 13,333
Totals			$101,667	$130,000	$113,333

(1) Allocated on the basis of 3,000 hours of computer usage.

(2) Allocated on the basis of 1,800 thousand square feet of floor space.

B.

1. The reciprocal allocation method allocates costs by including the services that the service departments provide each other. Thus, the overhead to be allocated includes each service department's direct costs as well as the costs of services obtained from the other service department. This method

provides a more accurate and equitable allocation of costs as costs are allocated using simultaneous equations.

2.   Theoretically, the reciprocal method would be appropriate in this situation. Since the Information Systems Department and the Facilities Department provide services to each other, there is a reciprocal relationship between the two. However, the reciprocal method is a more complex method. Therefore, it might be more efficient to use a simpler method even though the reciprocal allocation could easily be computed using a computer and an appropriate software package.

C.   Rather than allocating costs, Computer Information Services could assign the Information Systems (IS) Department's costs in several different ways, including the following:

- If the IS Department has the ability to keep track of actual computer usage time, as it seems to be able to do, then it would be more accurate, and perhaps simpler, to bill the production departments for each job or project based on actual hours used.

- The costs could be assigned through an activity-based costing (ABC) analysis.

Problem 5.7

A. The allocation of Sonimad Sawmill Inc.'s $1,000,000 joint processing costs to each of its three product lines under the three specified allocation methods is presented below.

1. Relative sales value method at split-off.

	Monthly Unit Output	Sales Price Per Unit	Relative Sales Value at Split-off	% of Sales	Allocated Joint Costs
Studs (Building)	75,000	$ 8	$ 600,000	46.15%	$ 461,539
Decorative Pieces	5,000	60	300,000	23.08	230,769
Posts	20,000	20	400,000	30.77	307,692
Totals			$1,300,000	100.00%	$1,000,000

2. Physical output (volume) method at split-off.

	Physical Unit Volume	% of Total Unit Volume	Allocated Joint Costs
Studs (Building)	75,000	75.00%	$ 750,000
Decorative Pieces	5,000	5.00	50,000
Posts	20,000	20.00	200,000
Totals	100,000	100.00%	$1,000,000

3. Estimated net realizable value method.

	Monthly Unit Output	Fully Processed Sales Price Per Unit	Estimated Net Realizable Value	% of Value	Allocated Joint Costs
Studs (Building)	75,000	$ 8	$ 600,000	44.44%	$ 444,445
Decorative Pieces	4,500 (1)	100		25.93	259,259
			350,000 (2)		
Posts	20,000	20	400,000	29.63	296,296
Totals			$1,350,000	100.00%	$1,000,000

Notes:

(1) 5,000 monthly units of output – 10% normal spoilage = 4,500 good units.

(2) 4,500 good units x $100 = $450,000 – further processing costs of $100,000 = $350,000.

B.   Presented below is an analysis for Sonimad Sawmill Inc. comparing the processing of decorative pieces further versus selling the rough-cut product immediately at split-off.

	Units	Dollars
Monthly unit output	5,000	
Less: Normal further processing shrinkage	500	
Units available for sale	4,500	
Final sales value (4,500 units @ $100 per unit)		$450,000
Less: Sales value at split-off		300,000
Differential revenue		150,000
Less: Further processing costs		100,000
Additional contribution from further processing		$ 50,000

Problem 5.8

A.

1.   The number of part-time employees for Quick Telephone Response (QTR) that will be needed each day using the regression results relating to the average number of daily orders handled is 19, calculated as follows:

$$E = a + bN$$
$$= 26.0265 + .0051 (3,450)$$
$$= 43.6215$$

Rounded to 44 total employees

44 total employees minus 25 full-time employees = 19 part-time employees

2.   The number of part-time employees that will be needed each day using the regression results relating to the average number of orders handled during the mid-day peak period is 17, calculated as follows:

$$E = a + bN$$
$$= 31.6785 + .0045 (2.250)$$
$$= 41.8035$$

Rounded to 42 total employees

42 total employees minus 25 full-time employees = 17 part-time employees

88

3.   Regression 2 is the better regression analysis of the two presented for the following reasons:

- Regression 2 has more economic plausibility than Regression 1. Since the peak demand occurs during the mid-day period, it is better to forecast the part-time workers based upon the mid-day orders.

- The standard error of the E estimate is lower for Regression 2 (4.228 versus 4.623), indicating that the predicted result is expected to be closer to the actual result. This measures the dispersion of the observed points around the estimated regression line.

- The coefficient of determination (r^2) is higher for Regression 2 (.682 versus .563), indicating that the independent variable predicts a higher proportion of the variance in the dependent variable. This means Regression 2 has a better "goodness of fit" than Regression 1.

B.   At least two ways that Weldon Miller could improve the regression predictions include the following:

- After the part-time operators begin processing orders, perform another regression analysis on the incremental orders handled by them versus the full-time operators. This would result in a more direct cause-and-effect relationship for the part-time and full-time operators.

- The analysis could be performed using multiple regression analysis. This could split the orders and data into those handled by the full-time employees and by the part-time employees during different period of the day. Other analyses could add factors such as the training period for new operators, seasonal issues in the mail-order business, or different levels of effort required to process different types of orders.

CHAPTER 6

Problem 6.1

A.   At least two reasons seem to have played an important role in highlighting the importance of allocating indirect costs in the past decade. These reasons are: (1) the increasing percentage of indirect costs, relative to total costs. This point is especially true in modern manufacturing firms, where automated operations have greatly shifted the cost structure in terms of direct and indirect costs; and (2) the recognition that a single cost driver usually is not an appropriate mechanism for allocating indirect costs.

B.   If your firm already has a clear picture of how indirect costs behave and should be allocated, the benefits of an ABC will likely be negligible.

      ABC tends to treat all indirect costs as variable costs.

      Other methods for allocating indirect costs via a multiple base approach may be more effective (e.g., regression models).

      The empirical evidence on the costs versus benefits of ABC systems is mixed.

Problem 6.2

Activity based management is the process by which a firm manages its activities. The goal is to manage these activities in a "reasonably efficient" manner. To accomplish this goal a firm needs to get a handle on the costs and benefits associated with its various activities, and ABC can be very helpful in this regard. However, ABC is but one of many ways for firms to get a handle on the costs of its activities. Indeed, long before ABC was ever discussed, many firms have been concerned about, and successful in, understanding the costs associated with individual activities.

Problem 6.3

Banks and libraries have various cost objectives to which indirect costs need to be allocated. ABC provides one meaningful way of allocating such costs. For example, if a bank is trying to determine the cost of processing a home mortgage, ABC provides a meaningful procedure for allocating indirect costs to that cost object. If a library is trying to determine the cost of providing reference services, ABC provides a meaningful procedure for allocating indirect costs to that cost objective. In both of the above examples, an ABC system would group the organization's indirect costs by activities and allocate such costs to the cost objective based on the appropriate cost driver.

Problem 6.4

The answer is a.

Problem 6.5

    a.   Since the indirect costs are all assumed to be variable in this problem, the total costs under a non-ABC system (no change) = Direct Materials + Direct Labor + Indirect Costs (overhead) = $25 + $15 + $10 = $50.

    b.   Total costs under the ABC system would also be $50 because the total indirect costs would still be allocated to the 18,000 bicycles regardless of the per unit driver event cost. More importantly, however, the only rationale for using the ABC system with the production of one product would be to get a better handle on the costs of specific activities.

Problem 6.6

A.   Activity-based costing (ABC) is a cost measurement system that focuses on the activities required to produce each product or service. After the required activities are identified, the resources consumed by the activities (i.e., costs) are measured and grouped into cost pools. The cause of these costs – called cost drivers – are identified and used as the basis of attaching costs to products and services.

Two examples of cost drivers that are not related to selling costs are setup costs and the number of material purchases for different types of yarn.

B.   Redwood Company's total selling cost for each order size and the per skein selling cost within each order size is calculated in Exhibit 4 below.

C.   The analysis of selling costs shows that small orders cost more than large orders. This could persuade management to market large orders more aggressively and/or offer discounts for large orders.

Exhibit 4

Redwood Company
Computations of Selling Costs
By Order Size and Per Skein Within Each Order Size

	Order Size			
	Small	Medium	Large	Total
Sales Commissions [1] ($675,000 / 2,700,000 = $.25/unit)	$ 6,000	$135,000	$ 534,000	$ 675,000
Catalogs [2] ($295,400 / 590,800 = $.50/catalog)	127,150	105,650	62,600	295,400
Catalog sales cost [3] ($105,000 / 175,000 = $.60/unit)	47,400	31,200	26,400	105,000
Credit & collection [4] ($60,000 / 6,000 = $10/order)	4,850	24,150	31,000	60,000
Total cost per order size	$185,400	$296,000	$ 654,000	$1,135,400
Divide by units sold	103,000	592,000	2,180,000	
Unit cost per order size	$1.80	$.50	$.30	

Notes:

[1] Retail sales in boxes x 12 skeins per box
x unit cost
   Small 2,000 x 12 x $.25
   Medium 45,000 x 12 x $.25
   Large 178,000 x 12 x $.25

[2] Catalogs distributed x unit cost

[3] Catalog sales in skeins x unit cost

[4] Number of retail orders x unit cost

Problem 6.7

A.

1. The calculation of total budgeted costs for the Manufacturing Department at Alyssa Manufacturing is presented below.

Direct material		
Tuff Stuff ($5.00 per unit x 20,000 units)	$100,000	
Ruff Stuff ($3.00 per unit x 20,000 units)	60,000	
Total direct material		$ 160,000
Direct labor		800,000
Overhead		
Indirect labor	$ 24,000	
Fringe benefits	5,000	
Indirect material	31,000	
Power	180,000	
Set-up	75,000	
Quality assurance	10,000	
Other utilities	10,000	
Depreciation	15,000	
Total overhead		350,000
Total Manufacturing Department budgeted cost		$1,310,000

2 & 3. The unit standard costs of Tuff Stuff and Ruff Stuff, with over-head allocated based on direct labor hours, are calculated as follows:

Tuff Stuff		
Direct material		$ 5.00
Direct labor [$8.00/hour x 2 hours (1)]		16.00
Overhead [$3.50/hour x 2 hours (1)]		7.00
Tuff Stuff unit standard cost		$ 28.00
Ruff Stuff		
Direct material		$ 3.00
Direct labor [$8.00/hour x 3 hours (1)]		24.00
Overhead [$3.50/hour x 3 hours (1)]		10.50
Ruff Stuff unit standard cost		$ 37.50
Note: (1)		
Budgeted direct labor hours		
Tuff Stuff 20,000 units x 2 hours		40,000
Ruff Stuff 20,000 units x 3 hours		60,000
Total budgeted direct labor hours		100,000
Direct labor rate $800,000/100,000 hours = $8.00/hour		
Overhead rate $350,000/100,000 hours = $3.50/hour		

B.

1. & 2.   The total budgeted cost of the Fabricating and Assembly Departments, after separation of overhead into the activity pools, is calculated as follows.

	Total	Fabricating		Assembly	
		Percent	Dollars	Percent	Dollars
Direct material	$ 160,000	100%	$160,000		
Direct labor	800,000	75%	600,000	25%	$200,000
Overhead					
Indirect labor	24,000	75%	18,000	25%	6,000
Fringe benefits	5,000	80%	4,000	20%	1,000
Indirect material	31,000		20,000		11,000
Power	180,000		160,000		20,000
Set-up	75,000		5,000		70,000
Quality assurance	10,000	80%	8,000	20%	2,000
Other utilities	10,000	50%	5,000	50%	5,000
Depreciation	15,000	80%	12,000	20%	3,000
Total overhead	350,000		232,000		118,000
Total budget	$1,310,000		$992,000		$318,000

C.

1. & 2.   The unit standard costs of the products using activity-based costing (ABC) are calculated below.

Fabricating Department	
Total cost	$992,000
Less: Direct material	160,000
Less: Direct labor	600,000
Pool overhead cost for allocation	$232,000
Hours: Tuff Stuff 4.4 hours x 20,000 units =	88,000
Ruff Stuff 6.0 hours x 20,000 units =	120,000
Total machine hours	208,000

Pool overhead cost per machine hour: $232,000 ÷ 208,000 = $1.1154/hour

Fabrication cost per unit: Tuff Stuff $1.1154 x 4.4 hours = $4.91 per unit
                            Ruff Stuff $1.1154 x 6.0 hours = $6.69 per unit

Assembly Department	
Total cost	$318,000
Less: Direct labor	200,000
Pool overhead cost for allocation	$118,000
Set-ups: Tuff Stuff	1,000
Ruff Stuff	272
Total set-ups	1,272

Pool cost per set-up: $118,000 ÷ 1,272 = $92.77 per set-up

Set-up cost per unit:
  Tuff Stuff $92.77 per set-up x 1,000 set-ups ÷
  20,000 units = $4.64 per unit
  Ruff Stuff $92.77 per set-up x 272 set-ups ÷ 20,000
  units = $1.26 per unit

Tuff Stuff Standard Cost	
Direct material	$ 5.00
Direct labor (2 hours x $8 per hour)	16.00
Fabrication Department overhead allocation	4.91
Assembly Department overhead allocation	4.64
Tuff Stuff unit standard cost	$30.55
Ruff Stuff Standard Cost	
Direct material	$ 3.00
Direct labor (3 hours x $8 per hour)	24.00
Fabrication Department overhead allocation	6.69
Assembly Department overhead allocation	1.26
Ruff Stuff unit standard cost	$34.95

Problem 6.8

A.   The allocation of all of Hawthorn company's budgeted manufacturing overhead based on direct labor hours, results in the unit manufacturing costs and unit sales prices for its three products, calculated as follows.

	Fuel Systems	Transmission Assemblies	Electrical Systems
Units	10,000	20,000	30,000
Standard labor hour/unit	2.0	1.5	1.0
Total standard labor hours	20,000	30,000	30,000
Direct material	$ 25.00	$ 36.00	$ 30.00
Direct labor at $10/hour	20.00	15.00	10.00
Overhead at $49/DLH [1]	98.00	73.50	49.00
Total cost	$143.00	$124.50	$ 89.00
Sales price at 125% of cost	$178.75	$155.63	$111.25

Note:

[1] Total manufacturing overhead of $3,920,000 ÷ 80,000 total direct labor hours = $49.00 per direct labor hour

B.   When the cost drivers, identified by Jim Briggs, are used to allocate manufacturing overhead, the unit manufacturing costs and unit sales prices for the three products manufactured at Hawthorn Company are calculated as follows.

	Fuel Systems	Transmission Assemblies	Electrical Systems
Units	10,000	20,000	30,000
Standard labor hour/unit	2.0	1.5	1.0
Total standard labor hours	20,000	30,000	30,000
Machine hours per unit	2.0	4.0	6.0
Total machine hours	20,000	80,000	180,000
Direct material	$ 25.00	$ 36.00	$ 30.00
Direct labor at $10/hour	20.00	15.00	10.00
Overhead – DLH at $7/hour [(1)]	14.00	10.50	7.00
Overhead – machine hours at $12/hour [(2)]	24.00	48.00	72.00
Total cost	$ 83.00	$109.50	$119.00
Sales price at 125% of cost	$103.75	$136.88	$148.75

Notes:

[(1)] Direct labor overhead of $560,000 ÷ 80,000 total direct labor hours = $7.00 per direct labor hour

[(2)] Machine overhead of $3,360,000 ÷ 280,000 total machine hours = $12.00 per machine hour

C. Presented below is a summary of the revised margins for each of Hawthorn Company's three products assuming the sales prices developed in Requirement A (allocation of all manufacturing overhead based on direct labor hours) is compared to revised costs developed in Requirement B (allocation of manufacturing overhead based on cost drivers).

	Fuel Systems	Transmission Assemblies	Electrical Systems
Current price	$178.75	$155.63	$111.25
Revised cost	83.00	109.50	119.00
Gross profit/(loss)	$ 95.75	$ 46.13	$ (7.75)
Margin	54%	30%	N/A

Based upon the above analysis, fuel systems and transmission assemblies are producing a higher return than Hawthorn Company previously thought. In particular, fuel systems are especially profitable with a 54 percent gross margin. The electrical systems, in contrast, are losing money on a full-cost basis.

Recommendations for improving profitability include the following.

- Increase emphasis on fuel systems, which could include increasing marketing expenditures and reducing the price to increase sales.

- Improve profitability of electrical systems, which could include improving the manufacturing process to reduce the machine hours required. Also, decrease marketing emphasis of this product, and increase the selling price if the market will bear it.

CHAPTER 7

Problem 7.1

A.   When prices are market driven, a firm still needs to determine whether it can sell the product at the market price and earn an acceptable level of profits. Such determination is essentially derived from cost accounting data.

B.   Target costing is a procedure for managing costs, such that, given a price, a desirable profit level is achieved. Firms that operate in environments where prices are largely market driven have used this approach long before the term "target costing" was coined. However, many believe that Japanese firms should be credited with using target costing in a dynamic fashion to improve cost management (i.e., via successive rounds of lowering costs).

Problem 7.2

a.   True
b.   False
c.   True
d.   True
e.   True

Problem 7.3

A.   Cost plus pricing approaches are based on earning a satisfactory level of profits rather than maximum profits. These approaches do not attempt to derive (in a mathematical sense) the cost and revenue functions required to maximize profits.

B.   No! Although a manager may begin by deriving a price based on some cost-plus formula, it is then incumbent upon the manager to assess whether the price derived is realistic given the market conditions confronting the product.

C. There are many reasons why firms use cost-plus pricing approaches, including the following:

1. They rely on accounting data which is readily available;

2. They permit firms to work toward a profit objective in an easily understood fashion, and

3. They provide a perception of fairness.

Problem 7.4

A. $P = \$100 - \$.2X$ (Constant slope of -.2)

$$TR = P \bullet X = \$100X - \$.2X^2$$

$$MR = \frac{dTR}{dx} = \$100 - \$.4X$$

Maximum Rev. is where $MR = 0$, thus:

$\$100 - \$.4X = 0; .4X = 100$

$X = 250; P = 100 - .2(250) = 50$

$$e_p = \frac{dx}{x} \bigg/ \frac{dP}{P} = \frac{dx}{dP} \bullet \frac{P}{x} = \frac{1}{\dfrac{dP}{dx}} \bullet \frac{P}{x} \qquad \text{(see footnote } ^{(1)}\text{)}$$

Therefore,

@ $X = 250, P = 50$

$$e_p = \frac{1}{-.2} \bullet \frac{50}{250} = -1 \text{ and } /e_p/ = 1$$

100

Although not required, it is interesting to examine $/e_p/$ at points below and above the output of $X = 200$.

For example, @ $X = 200$, $P = \$60$

$$e_p = \frac{1}{-.2} \bullet \frac{60}{200} = -1.5 \text{ and } /e_p/ = 1.5$$

@ $X = 300$, $P = \$40$

$$e_p = \frac{1}{-.2} \bullet \frac{40}{300} = -.667 \text{ and } /e_p/ = .667$$

---

[1] Alternatively, the demand function could be rewritten as:

$X = 500 - 5P$, and solve for e_p based on $\dfrac{dx}{dP} \bullet \dfrac{P}{x}$

B.   As shown in the example, profits are maximized where $X = 240$ and p $= \$52$. The $/e_p/$ at this point is:

$$e_p = \frac{1}{-.2} \bullet \frac{52}{240} = -1.083 \text{ and } /e_p/ = 1.083$$

Problem 7.5

Pros and cons noted below:

Pros

1.   New room revenues from 9 a.m. – 5 p.m. users;
2.   New revenues from meals served 9 a.m. – 5 p.m. users;
3.   Increased utilization of rooms will lower average fixed costs to all guests and could increase profits or reduce prices for overnight guests.

Cons

1.   Increased room utilization may cause some problems for having rooms ready for overnight guests.
2.   Increased staffing could create personnel related problems.

Problem 7.6

A.   The costs that will be relevant to Cathy Senna in the analysis of the special order being considered by Award Plus Co. are those expected future costs that are applicable to a particular decision (the costs that will differ between the alternatives of accepting or rejecting the offer). Only the variable costs of labor and materials are relevant. Since the order was received directly by Award Plus, variable marketing is not relevant because additional marketing costs will not be incurred under this order. The fixed costs are also not relevant because no additional capital investments are needed to meet the order; the firm is operating below full capacity and will be able to absorb this order.

B.   Award Plus Co. should accept the offer. Although the average unit
         cost of $148.75 is higher than the price offered, the unit incremental
         cost is only $85. Accepting the special order will result in a
         contribution per unit of $15 ($100 less $85) and a total additional
         contribution margin of $37,500 (2,500 units x $15), as shown below.

	Current Monthly Production	Special Order	Combined Production
Units produced	7,500	2,500	10,000
Sales	$1,312,500 (1)	$250,000 (2)	$1,562,500
Variable costs			
Labor	375,000	125,000 (3)	500,000
Materials	262,500	87,500 (4)	350,000
Marketing	187,500	--	187,500
Total variable costs	825,000	212,500	1,037,500
Fixed costs			
Manufacturing	275,000	--	275,000
Marketing	175,000	--	175,000
Total fixed costs	450,000	--	450,000
Total costs	1,275,000	212,500	1,487,500
Income before tax	$ 37,500	$ 37,500	$ 75,000
Costs per unit			
Variable (5)	$110.00	$85.00	$103.75
Fixed (6)	60.00	--	45.00
Average unit costs (7)	$170.00	$85.00	$148.75

(1) $175 x 7,500 units   = $1,312,500
(2) $100 x 2,500 units   = $ 250,000
(3) ($375,000 ÷ 7,500 units) x 2,500 units = $ 125,000
(4) ($262,500 ÷ 7,500 units) x 2,500 units = $ 87,500
(5) Total variable costs ÷ units produced = variable/incremental cost per unit
(6) Total fixed costs ÷ units produced   = fixed cost per unit
(7) Total costs ÷ units produced   = average cost per unit

Problem 7.7

A.   An analysis of relevant costs that shows whether or not the Midwest Division of Paibec Corporation should make MTR-2000 or purchase it from Marley Company for 2003 is as follows.

	Cost Per Unit	Total Cost for 32,000 Units
Cost to purchase MTR-2000 from Marley		
Bid price from Marley	$17.3000	$553,600
Equipment lease penalty (($36,000/12) x 2)	.1875	6,000
Total cost to purchase	$17.4875	$559,600
Cost for Midwest to make MTR-2000		
Direct material ($195,000/30,000 x 1.08)	$ 7.0200	$224,640
Direct labor ($120,000/30,000 x 1.05)	4.2000	134,400
Factory space rental ($84,000/32,000)	2.6250	84,000
Equipment leasing costs ($36,000/32,000)	1.1250	36,000
Variable manufacturing overhead (($225,000 x .4)/30,000)	3.0000	96,000
Fixed manufacturing overhead (not relevant)		
	---	---
Total cost to make	$17.9700	$575,040
Savings if purchased from Marley	$ .4825	$ 15,440

B.   Based solely on the financial results, the 32,000 units of MTR-2000 for 2003 should be purchased from Marley. The total cost from Marley would be $559,600, or $15,440 less than if the units were made by the Midwest Division.

Problem 7.8

A.   The downsizing plan would be acceptable as the required subsidy is less than 20 percent of the current subsidy; $15,000 compared to $16,700, calculated as follows.

Cost of downsizing plan:	
Wages and fringe benefits [(1)]	$ 81,250
Utilities and equipment maintenance	30,000
Annual cost of supplies [(2)]	96,250
Total costs	207,500
Annual revenue [(2)]	192,500
Mayfair downsizing plan subsidy	$ 15,000

[(1)] $65,000 + (25% x $65,000) = $81,250

[(2)] Annual revenue:
[(150 sandwiches x $3.60) + $230 beverages/desserts] x 250 days = $192,500
Cost of supplies: $192,500 x 50% = $ 96,250
Margin: $192,500 x 50% = $96,250

[(3)] Computation of subsidy limitation
Current operation

Cost of supplies ($210,000 x 60%)	$126,000
Wages [$110,000 + (25% x $110,000)]	137,500
Utilities & equipment maintenance	30,000
Total costs	293,500
Annual revenue [(4)]	210,000
Mayfair current operations subsidy	$ 83,500

Mayfair Corporation's subsidy limitation
20% of current subsidy (20% x $83,500) = $16,700

[(4)] [(100 entrees x $4) + (80 salads/sandwiches x $3) + $200 beverages/dessert] x 250 days

B.   The Wilco foods proposal is more advantageous to Mayfair
      Corporation than the downsizing plan as the subsidy at the projected
      volume is $5,140 less than the downsizing plan; $15,000 compared to
      $9,860.

Expected entrees:
  (50 x 40%) + (70 x 40%) + (90 x 20%) = 66 entrees

Revenue to Mayfair:
  Wilco revenue [1] $251,500
    Less: Breakeven sales [2]   48,000
    Revenues in excess of breakeven sales   203,500
  Revenues payable to Mayfair [3]   8,140
  Plus: Rent [4]   12,000
    Total payments to Mayfair   20,140

Cost of Mayfair:
  Fixed costs
    (Utilities and equipment maintenance)   30,000
    Mayfair's Wilco Foods proposal subsidy $ 9,860

[1] [(66 entrees x $5) + [(160 – 66) x $4] + $300] x 250 days
[2] ($1,000 monthly payment x 12 months) ÷ (1 – 75%) contribution margin
[3] Excess over breakeven sales x 4%
[4] $1,000 monthly payment x 12 months

CHAPTER 8

a. True
b. True
c. False
d. True
e. True
f. True
g. True

Problem 8.2

A. $RI = AP - (I \bullet K)$

B. $ROI = AP/I$

B.' $AP = ROI \bullet I$
      Substitute B' into A

A.' $RI = (ROI \bullet I) - (I \bullet K)$
      $= (ROI - K) \bullet I$

Problem 8.3

A. $\$700,000 - (K \bullet \$3,500,000) = \$950,000 - (K \bullet \$5,000,000)$

      $K (\$1,500,000) = \$250,000$

      $$K = \frac{250,000}{1,500,000}$$

      $K = 16 \ 2/3\%$

B.   Although not explicitly required, the graph provided below is helpful
      in answering part B of this problem.

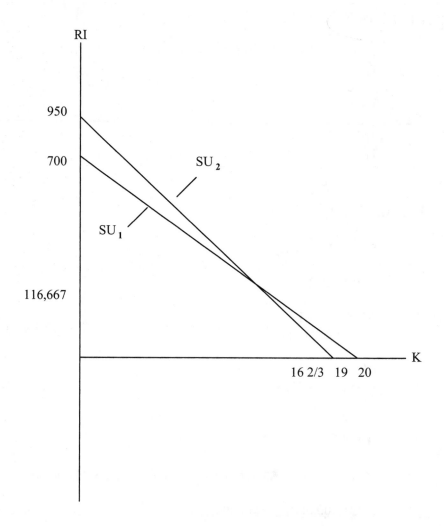

SU$_1$ has an ROI of 20% and seems to be doing better than SU$_2$.
However, if SU$_1$ had the differential investment of $250,000 (i.e.,
950,000 – 700,000) and could not earn at least 16 2/3% on this extra
investment, then SU$_2$ would be doing a better job of performance.

Problem 8.4

A. *Strengths:*

      1.   Financial performance measures are relatively objective due to their quantitative nature.

      2.   Since financial measures are quantitative, they permit easy comparisons within and across firms.

      3.   In the final analysis, a firm's survival is dependent upon successful financial performance. Hence, financial performance measures provide a direct link to long-run survival.

    Weaknesses:

      1.   The relationship between financial performance measures and many nonfinancial performance indicators (e.g., quality, customer satisfaction) is often difficult to assess, especially in the short-run.

      2.   Many argue that financial performance measures are "lagging" indicators of firm performance (see B below).

B. The production cycle (or supply chain) of an organization can be thought of in terms of inputs, processes, and outputs. Financial performance measures tend to focus on comparing the financial value of outputs to the financial costs of inputs, which means there is usually a lag effect in the evaluation process. It is interesting to note that this lag may be substantially reduced in some internet based firms. However, as noted in the chapter, for these very same firms the traditional financial performance measures (e.g., profits) often develop even a greater lag in signaling long-term survivability of a firm.

Problem 8.5

A.   The theoretical justification for residual income is that the present value of future residual income (discounted at the firm's cost of capital) is equal to a firm's net present value. Market value added is also equal to the firm's net present value (providing the market value of the firm is properly assessed. Thus, the present value of the firm's residual income and its market value added are both proxies for the present value of the firm's future cash flows.

B.   Economic value added (which is a stylized version of residual income) is not a true measure of periodic economic value. Market value added is only as good as is the market's estimates of the firm's equity and debt.

Problem 8.6

A.   The use of incentive compensation packages in the U.S. for CEO's has been spurred by the concern for agency conflicts between stockholders and top management. The type of incentive plans put in place over the past two decades usually have a large component based on stock options. The increase in the overall U.S. stock market value over this time period has resulted in significant incentive payments to the CEO's.

B.   No. The key issue here is whether there is a strong relationship between pay and performance for CEO's. Recent studies that properly consider the dynamic nature of the pay-performance issue show a strong correlation (e.g., see Boschen and Smith (1995)). Of course, the fact that CEO pay and performance are highly correlated for a sample of firms does not mean that there are not some specific exceptions.

Problem 8.7

A.

Division A	Division B
RI = AP − [(K) (I)] $600,000 = AP − [(15\%) (\$2,000,000)]$ AP = $900,000* $ROI = \dfrac{\$\ 900,000}{\$2,000,000} = 45\%$	RI = AP − [(K) (I)] RI = (ROI − K) I $750,000 = (45\% - 15\%)$ I $\dfrac{\$750,000}{30\%} = I$ I = $2,500,000 AP = ROI(I) AP = 45% ($2,500,000) = $1,125,000*

B. Since the two divisions are earning the same return on investment (ROI) of 45%, the answer to this question boils down to what would happen if Division A had the extra $500,000 investment (i.e., $2,500,000 - $2,000,000), rather than Division B. It should be noted that the extra $150,000 in residual income being earned by Division B is due to its ability to earn 45% on all of its investments. If it is assumed that the reason Division B has the extra $500,000 in investments is because it could better utilize such investments, then the argument would fall in favor of promoting the manager of Division B. Alternatively, if a case could be made that Division A could earn more than 45% on the extra $500,000 investment, then the manager of Division A should be promoted.

111

Problem 8.8

A.   At least three problems that Domi Products could encounter when using return on assets (ROA) as the basis of performance measurement include:

- Difficulty in determining the appropriate asset value; book value may not be very useful, since the rate of return artificially increases as assets get older.

- Possibly rejecting profitable projects

- Segment managers delaying the replacement of old and inefficient assets unless current replacement cost is used as the asset value. A new asset increases the asset base and, thus, decreases ROA resulting in negative, long-run consequences.

B.

1.   **Residual income (RI)** is defined as the division's operating income (segment margin) after deducting a charge for imputed interest. Imputed interest is equal to the asset used by the division multiplied by the firm's cost of capital.

2.   RI should be adopted as it reveals the firm's true cost of capital to managers, and avoids many of the problems of the ROA approach. However, a different interest charge for each division may be necessary, as well as a more uniform accounting method and/or asset base, particularly if the divisions use different accounting methods that cause significant asset variations (e.g., accelerated vs. straight line depreciation).

C.

1.   The beneficial behavioral implications of division managers participating in the corporate budgeting development process include:

- Goals being more realistic and acceptable and, therefore, the evaluation is perceived as fair.

- Improvement in communication, coordination, and group cohesion.

- A sense of commitment and willingness to be held accountable/responsible for the budget.

2.   The decision to more equitably allocate common costs should motivate managers. However, any cost allocation is likely to be somewhat subjective and, thus, could lead to negative behavioral consequences.

CHAPTER 9

Problem 9.1

  a. False
  b. True
  c. True
  d. True
  e. False
  f. True
  g. True

Problem 9.2

A.   *Pros*

  - Nonfinancial measures tend to lead financial measures (i.e., cause-effect relationship)

  - Nonfinancial measures are often a signal to long-run success

  Cons

  - In the long-run, the success of a firm needs to be judged in financial terms (i.e., a bankrupt firm is not a successful firm).

  - Nonfinancial measures often lack reliability

B.   There is no easy way to weigh the different measures. Thus, if the two sets of measures signal different performance (e.g., financial measures signal good performance and nonfinancial measures signal poor performance), there is no simple way to reconcile this difference.

Problem 9.3

A.   Product quality refers to the dependability of a product. Percentage of defective products is a way to measure product quality (i.e., the lower the percentage, the higher the quality).

B.   Customer satisfaction refers to the attitude customers have toward a company's products. Customer satisfaction can be measured by percentage of returns (i.e., lower is better) or through surveys.

C.   Productivity is a measure of efficiency and usually measured as a ratio of outputs to inputs.

D.   Market share is the percentage of the industry sales attributed to a firm. It is measured by dividing the firm's sales by the industry's sales.

Problem 9.4

The three-way classification scheme discussed in Chapter 1 is based on financial/nonfinancial, ex post/ex ante, and internal/external dimensions of information and provides a database design approach that is consistent with the balanced scorecard philosophy of considering financial and nonfinancial measures of performance.

Problem 9.5

A.   Ask managers in a firm to list key financial and nonfinancial measures.

B.   Have managers weight each measure.

C.   Ask managers to discuss compensatory vs. noncompensatory aspects of weighted measures.

Problem 9.6

Ask students to carefully examine the publicly available data for General Electric Corp.

Problem 9.7

A.   In the long-run, corporate earnings drive cash flows, which drive firm value. However, in the short-run, it seems reasonable for other factors, especially sales growth, to be a key signal for sustained earnings. In essence, the market place seems to be saying that these other factors will ultimately translate into sustained earnings which in turn translate into sustained market value. The earnings will have to materialize if the firm's market value is to be maintained.

B.   As discussed in the chapter, there are many who believe that nonfinancial measures are leading indicators of firm performance. Hence, if a relationship exists between nonfinancial measures and earnings (and/or market value), these nonfinancial measures could be used to explain why the market value of a firm is increasing even though earnings are lagging behind.

Problem 9.8

A.   At least three of the several factors that should be present for an organization's quality program to be successful include:

- Evidence of top management support, including motivational leadership and resource commitments.

- Training of those affected, including employees and suppliers.

- A cultural change leading to a corporate culture committed to the customer and to continuous, dynamic improvement.

B.   From an analysis of the Cost of Quality Report, it would appear that Bergen Inc.'s program has been successful since:

- Total quality costs as a percentage of total production have declined from 23.4 percent to 13.1 percent.

- External failure costs, those costs signaling customer dissatisfaction, have declined from 8 percent of total production to 2.3 percent. These declines in warranty repairs and customer returns should translate into increased sales in the future.

116

- Internal failure costs have been reduced from 4.6 percent to 2.2 percent of production costs and the overall cost of scrap and rework has gone down by 45.7 percent.

- Appraisal costs have decreased 43.4 percent. Higher quality is reducing the demand for final testing.

- Quality costs have shifted to the area of prevention where problems are solved before the customer becomes involved. Maintenance, training, and design reviews have increased from 5.8 percent of total production to 6 percent and from 25 percent of total quality costs to 45.7 percent. The $30,000 increase is more than offset by decreases in other quality costs.

C.   Tony Reese's current reaction to the quality improvement program is more favorable as he is seeing the benefits of having the quality problems investigated and solved before they reach the production floor. Because of improved designs, quality training, and additional pre-production inspections, scrap and rework costs have declined. Production does not have to spend an inordinate amount of time with customer service since they are now making the product right the first time. Throughput has increased and throughput time has decreased; work is now moving much faster through the department.

D.   To measure the opportunity cost of not implementing the quality program, Bergen Inc. could assume that:

- Sales and market share would continue to decline and then calculate the revenue and income lost;

- The company would have to compete on price rather than quality and calculate the impact of having to lower product prices.

CHAPTER 10

Problem 10.1

A.   **Negotiated transfer** price is a transfer price derived through negotiations between the buying and selling subunits. **Market based** transfer is a transfer price derived from the price charged by an external market supplier. **Cost based** transfer price is a transfer price derived from the costs of the intermediate product.

B.   Yes, when the external market for the intermediate product is perfectly competitive, the market based transfer price usually dominates other methods. Under such a condition, the selling subunit could sell outside as many units as it wishes at the market price and the buying subunit could buy as many units as it wishes at the same price. Hence, even if negotiations were to take place, it is reasonable to expect both subunits to settle on a transfer price which is equal to (or slightly modified due to transaction cost savings) the external market price.

C.   Corporate tax rates vary significantly across countries. A key corporate strategy is to minimize taxes on profits. In general, global corporate taxes are reduced and net profits increased when subunit profits are shifted from high taxing countries to low taxing countries. The amount of profits recorded in one country over another is in part determined by the transfer pricing technique used. Thus, transfer pricing is one possible way (subject to the tax laws of the countries involved) of causing such a shift in profits.

Problem 10.2

    a.   True
    b.   False
    c.   False
    d.   False
    e.   True
    f.   False
    g.   False

Problem 10.3

There is no simple answer to this question. As long as the computer facilities are not fully utilized, variable costing would help encourage greater usage of the facilities. However, in the long-run (which may not be very far into the future), the computer facilities need to be replaced. Hence, an argument for full costs may be quite valid. Of course, given the problems associated with a simple cost recovery transfer pricing system (discussed in the chapter), a cost-plus system may be preferred. However, even a cost-plus system raises serious problems. Finally, if the Computer Center could sell its services outside the University, then (again depending on capacity utilization) an argument for opportunity costs may become dominant.

Problem 10.4

Banks, libraries, and hospitals have numerous internal transfers of services from one subunit to another. Thus, the amount charged (i.e., the transfer price) for the transferred services will partially determine the performance of those subunits being treated as profit or investment centers. In addition, the level of services by particular subunits, and the organization as a whole, will also be affected by transfer prices.

Problem 10.5

A.   Among the reasons transfer prices based on cost are not appropriate as a divisional performance measure are because they:

- Provide little incentive for the selling division to control manufacturing costs as all costs incurred will be recovered;

- Often lead to suboptimal decisions for the company as a whole.

B.   Using the market price as the transfer price, the contribution margin for both the Mining Division and the Metals Division for the year ended May 31, 2003, is as calculated in Exhibit 1 below.

Exhibit 1

Ajax Consolidated Calculation of
Divisional Contribution Margin
For the Year Ended May 31, 2003

	Mining Division	Metals Division
Selling Price	$ 90	$ 150
Less: Variable costs		
Direct material	12	6
Direct labor	16	20
Manufacturing overhead		
	24 [1]	10 [2]
Transfer price	---	90
Unit contribution margin	$ 38	$ 24
Volume	x 400,000	x 400,000
Total contribution margin	$15,200,000	$9,600,000

[1] Variable overhead = $32 x 75% = $24

[2] Variable overhead = $25 x 40% = $10

Note:
The $5 variable selling cost that the Mining Division would incur for sales on the open market should not be included as this is an internal transfer.

C.   If the use of a negotiated transfer price was instituted by Ajax Consolidated, which also permitted the divisions to buy and sell on the open market, the price range for toldine that would be acceptable to both divisions would be determined as follows:

The Mining Division would like to sell to the Metals Division for the same price it can obtain on the outside market, $90 per unit. However, Mining would be willing to sell the toldine for $85 per unit as the $5 variable selling cost would be avoided.

The Metals Division would like to continue paying the bargain price of $66 per unit. However, if Mining does not sell to Metals, Metals would be forced to pay $90 on the open market. Therefore, Metals would be satisfied to receive a price concession from Mining equal to the costs that Mining would avoid by selling internally. Therefore, a negotiated transfer price for toldine between $85 and $90 would benefit both divisions and the company as a whole.

D. A negotiated transfer price is the most likely to elicit desirable management behavior as it will:

- Encourage the management of the Mining Division to be more conscious of cost control;
- Benefit the Metals Division by providing toldine at less cost than its competitors;
- Provide a more realistic measure of divisional performance.

Problem 10.6

A. This part of the problem lends itself to an open ended class discussion on the different effects transfer pricing can have on opening a subunit (e.g., a manufacturing plant) in one country vs. another country. The best way to summarize the issues involved would be to first identify the key components of each specific issue involved. The issues which need discussion are:

1. Minimizing corporate taxes;
2. Problems associated with foreign currency translations;
3. Assessing political risk and the impact of such risk on expected cash flows;
4. The cost of raising capital in the host and home country;
5. The trade-off between labor costs, efficiency and quality;
6. The strategic gain, if any, for the firm to have presence in Africa and/or Asia.

B. Once the above issues have been discussed, it may be possible to rank in descending order the importance afforded to each issue. Once the issues are clearly identified and rank-ordered, it becomes a managerial decision as to the method of trading off the pros and cons of the various concerns.

CHAPTER 11

Problem 11.1

A.   The operating budget provides a formal plan for current operating activities, with emphasis on forecasting revenues and expenses. Having such a plan helps direct a firm toward achieving its operating goals. It also helps a firm better understand how to improve its performance in future periods via the comparison of actual results with past expectations. Finally, operating budgets also can play an important role in motivating individuals to achieve target levels of performance.

B.   The cash flow budget provides a plan for cash flows. The cash flow budget plays an important role in assuring that a firm will not have its activities interrupted due to cash shortages. At the same time, the cash flow budget helps a firm minimize the likelihood of having excessive cash on hand.

Problem 11.2

A.   Proper cash management is essential to all firms. However, it does not follow that periodic cash flows provide a good measure of firm performance or firm value. Cash flows are quite "lumpy" from period to period due to the timing of actual cash collections and payments. As a result, periodic cash flows are not good measures of periodic firm performance. In contrast, accrual accounting earnings reduce much of this "lumpiness" via the process of matching earned revenues with incurred expenses. Hence, accrual accounting earnings are not only a better periodic performance measure than cash flows, but they also do a better job of predicting future cash flows and, in turn, firm value.

B.   The difference between accounting income from operations and cash flows from operations is essentially the difference between the accrual process of recording earnings and expenses versus the cash flow process of recording the same. Although depreciation (plus amortization and depletion) accounts for an important part of this difference, there are many other accrual items which need to be considered. For example, timing of cash collections from sales, the timing of cash payments of expenses, and the timing of tax payments. These other items can easily affect the difference between operating income and cash flows by as much, if not more, than depreciation (plus amortization and depletion).

Problem 11.3

The mixed findings regarding the effect of budgeting on performance is not so surprising in light of the fact that many factors (both financial and non-financial) affect the relationship between budgets and motivation. The way to reconcile these mixed findings is to place the studies in the context of a theory of motivation. One such theory is known as "expectancy theory." Based on expectancy theory, Ronen and Livingstone (1975) were able to provide insight into unraveling the confusing findings. In particular, they showed that budgets effect the motivation of individuals in terms of intrinsic and extrinsic rewards, as well as in terms of the probabilities individuals assign to achieving goals and receiving rewards.

Problem 11.4

The pro forma cash budget for Alpha-Tech for the second quarter of 2004 is presented below. Supporting calculations are presented on the next page.

<table>
<tr><th colspan="4">Alpha-Tech
Cash Budget for the Second Quarter 2004</th></tr>
<tr><th></th><th>April</th><th>May</th><th>June</th></tr>
<tr><td>Beginning balance</td><td>$ 500,000</td><td>$ 500,000</td><td>$ 1,230,000</td></tr>
<tr><td>Collections [1]</td><td></td><td></td><td></td></tr>
<tr><td>February sales</td><td>4,000,000</td><td></td><td></td></tr>
<tr><td>March sales</td><td>5,400,000</td><td>3,600,000</td><td></td></tr>
<tr><td>April sales</td><td>---</td><td>6,900,000</td><td>4,600,000</td></tr>
<tr><td>May sales</td><td>---</td><td>---</td><td>7,500,000</td></tr>
<tr><td>Total receipts</td><td>9,400,000</td><td>10,500,000</td><td>12,100,000</td></tr>
<tr><td>Total cash available</td><td>9,900,000</td><td>11,000,000</td><td>13,330,000</td></tr>
<tr><td>Disbursements</td><td></td><td></td><td></td></tr>
<tr><td>Accounts payable</td><td>4,155,000</td><td>4,735,000</td><td>5,285,000</td></tr>
<tr><td>Wages [2]</td><td>3,450,000</td><td>3,750,000</td><td>4,200,000</td></tr>
<tr><td>General & administrative [3]</td><td>900,000</td><td>900,000</td><td>900,000</td></tr>
<tr><td>Property taxes</td><td>---</td><td>---</td><td>340,000</td></tr>
<tr><td>Income taxes [4]</td><td>1,280,000</td><td>---</td><td>---</td></tr>
<tr><td>Total disbursements</td><td>$9,785,000</td><td>$ 9,385,000</td><td>$10,725,000</td></tr>
<tr><td>Cash balance</td><td>115,000</td><td>1,615,000</td><td>2,605,000</td></tr>
<tr><td>Cash borrowed</td><td>385,000</td><td>---</td><td>---</td></tr>
<tr><td>Cash repaid</td><td>---</td><td>(385,000)</td><td>---</td></tr>
<tr><td>Ending balance</td><td>$ 500,000</td><td>$ 1,230,000</td><td>$ 2,605,000</td></tr>
</table>

[1] 60% of sales in first month; 40% of sales in second month.

[2] 30% of current month sales.

[3] (Total less property taxes and depreciation) ÷ 12.

[4] 40% x $3,200,000.

Problem 11.5

A.

1. The semi-annual installments and total bonus for the Charter Division are calculated as follows:

Charter Division Bonus Calculation for Year Ended September 30, 2004		
October 2003 – March 2004		
Profitability	(.02) ($462,000)	$ 9,240
Rework	(.02 x $462,000) - $11,500	(2,260)
On-time delivery	No bonus – under 96%	-0-
Sales returns	[(.015 x $4,200,000 - $84,000] x 50%	(10,500)
Semi-annual installment		(3,520)
Semi-annual bonus awarded		-0 -
April 2004 – September 2004		
Profitability	(.02) ($440,000)	8,800
Rework	(.02 x $440,000) - $11,000	(2,200)
On-time delivery	96%-98%	2,000
Sales returns	[(.015 x $4,400,000) - $70,000] x 50%	(2,000)
Semi-annual installment		6,600
Semi-annual bonus awarded		6,600
Total bonus awarded for the year		$ 6,600

2. The manager of the charter Division is likely to be frustrated by the new plan as the division bonus is more than $20,000 less than the previous year when sales and operating income were similar. However, both on-time deliveries and sales returns improved in the second half of the year while rework costs were relatively even. If the division continues to improve at the same rate, the Charter bonus will approximate or exceed what it was under the old plan. The only open question is whether or not the manager has sufficient motivation to effect improvement.

B.

1. The semi-annual installments and total bonus for the Mesa Division are calculated as follows:

Mesa Division Bonus Calculation for Year Ended September 30, 2004		
October 2003 – March 2004		
Profitability	(.02) ($342,000)	$ 6,840
Rework	(.02 x $342,000) - $6,000	-0-
On-time delivery	Over 98%	5,000
Sales returns	[(.015 x $2,850,000 - $44,750] x 50%	(1,000)
Semi-annual installment		10,840
April 2004 – September 2004		
Profitability	(.02) ($406,000)	8,120
Rework	(.02 x $406,000) - $8,000	-0-
On-time delivery	No bonus – under 96%	-0-
Sales returns	[(.015 x $2,900,000) - $42,500] x 50%	3,000
Semi-annual installment		11,120
Total bonus awarded for the year		$ 21,960

2. The manager of the Mesa Division should be as satisfied with the new plan as with the old plan as the bonus was almost equivalent. However, there is no sign of improvements in this division; as a matter of fact, on-time deliveries declined considerably in the second half of the year. Unless the manager institutes better controls, the bonus situation may not be as favorable in the future in which case he will become dissatisfied. This could motivate the manager to improve, or it could demotivate him if he is frustrated.

C. Ben Harrington's revised bonus plan for the Charter Division fostered improvements including a(n):

- Increase of 1.9 percent in on-time deliveries;
- $500 reduction in rework costs;
- $14,000 reduction in sales returns.

However, operating income as a percent of sales (11 to 10 percent) has decreased.

The Mesa Division's bonus has remained at the status quo as the effects of the revised plan at Summit Equipment have been offset with a(n):

- Increase of 2.0 percent in operating income as a percent of sales (12 to 14 percent);
- Decrease of 3.6 percent in on-time deliveries;
- $2,000 increase in rework costs;
- $2,250 decrease in sales returns.

This would suggest that there needs to be some revisions to the bonus plan. Several suggestions include:

- A reward structure for rework costs that are below 2 percent of operating income that would encourage managers to drive costs lower.

- Reviewing the whole year in total. The bonus plan should carry forward the negative amounts for one six-month period into the next six-month period incorporating the entire year when calculating a bonus.

- Developing benchmarks, and then giving rewards for improvements over prior periods and encouraging continuous improvement.

Problem 11.6

A.   The cash that TabComp Inc. can expect to collect during April 2004 is calculated below.

April cash receipts:	
April cash sales ($400,000 x .25)	$100,000
April credit card sales ($400,000 x .30 x .96)	115,200
Collections on account:	
March ($480,000 x .45 x .70)	151,200
February ($500,000 x .45 x .28)	63,000
January (uncollectible – not relevant)	0
Total collections	$429,400

B.

    1.   The projected number of the MZB-33 computer hardware units that TabComp Inc. will order on January 25, 2004, is calculated as follows.

	MZB-33 Units
March sales	110
Plus: Ending inventory [(1)]	27
Total needed	137
Less: Beginning inventory [(2)]	33
Projected purchases in units	104

[(1)] .30 x 90 unit sales in April

[(2)] .30 x 110 unit sales in March

    2.

Purchase price = $3,000 selling price per unit [(3)]	
x 60%	$ 1,800
x Projected unit purchases	104
Value of MZB-33 purchases	$187,200

[(3)] Selling price = $2,025,000 ÷ 675 units = $3,000 per unit

    3.   Assuming TabComp Inc. pays according to the terms of n/45, these computer hardware units will be paid for in April. The units were ordered on January 25; there is a one-month lead time required for delivery; and payment will be made on the last day of the 45-day discount period.

Problem 11.7

A.   Following are the monthly budgets for Bullen & Company for the first quarter of 2004.

	January	February	March	Quarter
1. Production budget (units)				
Sales units	20,000	24,000	16,000	60,000
Plus: ending inventory	12,000	8,000	9,000	9,000
Total units required	32,000	32,000	25,000	69,000
Less: beginning inventory	10,000	12,000	8,000	10,000
Units to be produced	22,000	20,000	17,000	59,000
2. Direct labor budget (hours)				
Units to be produced	22,000	20,000	17,000	59,000
Direct labor hours per unit	4.0	4.0	3.5	
Total labor budget (hours)	88,000	80,000	59,500	227,500
3. Direct materials budget (dollars)				
Units to be produced	22,000	20,000	17,000	59,000
Cost per unit	$ 10	$ 10	$ 10	$ 10
Total direct materials cost	$ 220,000	$ 200,000	$ 170,000	$ 590,000
4. Sales budget (dollars)				
Sales units	20,000	24,000	16,000	60,000
Sales price per unit	$ 80	$ 80	$ 75	
Total sales revenue budget	$1,600,000	$1,920,000	$1,200,000	$4,720,000

B.   The total budgeted contribution margin for Bullen & Company for the
      first quarter of 2004 would be calculated as follows.

Bullen & Company				
Budgeted Contribution Margin				
First Quarter, 2004				
	January	February	March	Quarter
Direct labor hours per unit	4.0	4.0	3.5	
Direct labor hourly rate	$15	$15	$16	
Direct labor cost per unit	$60	$60	$56	
Sales units	20,000	24,000	16,000	60,000
Sales revenue	$1,600,000	$1,920,000	$1,200,000	$4,720,000
Direct labor cost	1,200,000	1,440,000	896,000	3,536,000
Material cost	200,000	240,000	160,000	600,000
Contribution margin	$ 200,000	$ 240,000	$ 144,000	$ 584,000

Problem 11.8

a. True
b. True
c. False
d. True
e. False
f. True
g. True

CHAPTER 12

Problem 12.1

Sophisticated methods of capital budgeting are probably used more in some countries than other countries for several reasons, some of which are listed below:

1. The political and economic uncertainties impacting future cash flows are, generally speaking, lower in some countries than other countries. Thus, forecasting cash flows from capital expenditures is likely a more realistic process (on a relative basis) in firms within these countries.

2. Sophisticated capital budgeting techniques rely on risk-adjusted discounted cash flows. The proper discount rate is itself dependent on the assumption of a reasonably efficient capital market. In some countries, this assumption is appropriate, whereas in other countries the notion of efficient capital markets is quite far from reality.

3. Sophisticated methods of capital budgeting focus on financial measures of performance. In some countries, this focus dominates, whereas in other countries nonfinancial concerns seem to dominate.

Problem 12.2

There are many ways to modify the example given on pages 284-286. That would answer the two questions posed. One simple solution for each question is to change the cost of the investment, shown below.

A. If the cost of the investment were only $2,000,000, instead of $8,000,000, then it pays to invest now. In this case the NPV of the investment today is $6,971,836 and the option value associated with deferring the investment is only $1,069,252 [i.e., (9,649,306/1.2)-($6,971,836)].

B.   If the cost of the investment were $12,000,000, instead of $8,000,000, then it would never pay to make this investment. In this case the NPV of the investment is less than zero both today and if the investment were deferred.

Problem 12.3

Strategic planning is concerned with the long-term positioning, and related commitments, of the organization. Capital budgeting is concerned with capital investments (i.e., expenditures which are intended to benefit the firm for several operating periods). In essence, capital investments represent the commitment aspect of strategic plans.

Problem 12.4

Intellectual capital refers to the intangible knowledge assets of a firm. However, these assets are neither shown on the balance sheet nor are they amortized on the income statement. Nevertheless, a well recognized aspect of many firms operating in the new information economy is the fact that knowledge assets are key, if not the key, assets owned by these firms. As such, managing these assets (i.e., knowledge management) is of critical importance to these firms.

Conceptually, investments in intellectual capital should be made in a manner similar to any other asset. That is, the present value of future cash flows should be compared to the cost of the asset. Operationally, it is usually quite difficult to quantify the long-term benefits of such assets. Accordingly, and somewhat unfortunately, it is not common for firms to treat investments in intellectual capital as if they were capital investments.

Problem 12.5

The answer is d.

Problem 12.6

A.

1.   The payback method measures the period of time it will take to recoup, in the form of net cash inflows, the net dollar investment in the project. This method is of particular interest when projects are considered risky. Management usually establishes a maximum payback period, generally in years. Projects with paybacks that are equal to or less than the required payback period are considered acceptable. Several benefits and limitations of the payback method include the following.

Benefits – The payback method
- is simple to compute and understand.
- emphasizes the return of capital, rather than return on capital.

Limitations – The payback method does not
- recognize the time value of money.
- take into consideration cash flows beyond the payback period.

2.   Calculation of the payback periods for each of the four projects are presented below.

Calculation of Dollar Returns to Reach Years of Payback (in thousands of dollars)			
Project	Annual Cash Flows	Payback Period	Initial Investment
A	$50 + $50 + $50 + $50 =	4.0 years	$200
B	$40 + $50 + $70 + ($30 ÷ $75) =	3.4 years	$190
C	$75 + $75 + $60 + ($40 ÷ $80) =	3.5 years	$250
D	$75 + $75 + $60 =	3.0 years	$210

133

B.

    1.   The calculation of the net present value for each project is presented below.

Net present value = Equipment cost – the present value of the aggregate cash flow.					
Period	Present Value of $1	Project A	Project B	Project C	Project D
1	0.893	$ 44,650	$ 35,720	$ 66,975	$ 66,975
2	0.797	39,850	39,850	59,775	59,775
3	0.712	35,600	49,840	42,720	42,720
4	0.636	31,800	47,700	50,880	25,440
5	0.567	28,350	42,525	56,700	11,340
Present value of cash inflows		180,250	215,635	277,050	206,250
Equipment cost		200,000	190,000	250,000	210,000
Net present value		$(19,750)	$ 25,635	$ 27,050	$ (3,750)

    2.   The excess present value index (profitability index) is equal to the present value of cash inflows divided by the cost of the equipment. The calculated excess present value indexes, by project, are presented below.

Project A	Project B	Project C	Project D
90.1%	113.5%	110.8%	98.2%

C.   Assuming venture capital funds can be obtained, it is recommended that Projects B and C be funded. Both of these projects have positive net present values and excess present value indexes greater than 100 percent.

Problem 12.7

A.   **Accounting Rate of Return**
The merits of the accounting rate of return (ARR) method are that the method is relatively simple to use and easy to understand. It considers the profitability of the projects under consideration. The limitations of the ARR method include ignoring cash flows and the time value of money.

Internal Rate of Return
The merits of the internal rate of return (IRR) method are that it considers the time value of money and measures the true economic return of the project and productivity of the capital invested in the project. The limitations of the IRR method are that the answer is stated as a percentage rather than a dollar amount, making it more difficult to understand and explain to management. The IRR method also unrealistically assumes that cash flows are reinvested at the IRR of the project.

Net Present Value Method
The merits of the net present value (NPV) method are that it considers the time value of money and size of the investment. The NPV method measures the true economic return of the project, the productivity of the capital investment, and the change in the organization's shareholders' wealth. The limitations of the NPV method include the assumption that all cash flows are reinvested at the discount (hurdle) rate, and it does not calculate a project's rate of return.

Payback Method
The merits of the payback method are that it considers cash flows and provides a measure of the liquidity and risk of the investment. The limitations of the payback method are that it neglects the time value of money and the project's profitability.

B.   Miranda Wells and Jake Richter are basing their judgment on the results of the net present value and internal rate of return calculations. These are both considered better measures because they include cash flows, the time value of money, and the project's profitability. Project B is better than Project A for both of these measures.

C. At least three qualitative considerations that should generally be considered in capital budget evaluations include the following.

- Quicker response to market changes and flexibility in production capacity.
- Strategic fit and long-term competitive improvements from the project, or the negative impact to the company's competitiveness or image if it does not make the investment.
- Risks inherent in the project, business, or country for the investment.

Problem 12.8

The answer is c.

Initial Investment		($100,000)
Annual Cash Income	$70,000	
Annual Cash Expenses	20,000	
Net Operating Inflows	50,000	
Taxes ($50,000 @ 40%)	20,000	
Net After Taxes	30,000	
Present Value of Net After Taxes		
(3.605 x $30,000)		108,150
Present Value of Annual Depreciation Tax		
Savings ($100,000 x 40% x 3.605)		28,840
Net Present Value of Investment		$136,990

Problem 12.9

In principle, this problem can be considered via a NPV analysis. The initial cost of the four consultants (i.e., $440,000), plus the indirect costs (i.e., $100,000), would represent the initial investments. At this point, however, the problem becomes more difficult. The real issue in this problem revolves around the appropriate amount of cash flows (which are derived from the estimated revenues) to use in the analysis. As the Director freely admits, the initial estimates are far from accurate.

One way to approach this problem is do a simulation based on the cash flow possibilities, for a four-year time horizon. What will become apparent from such a simulation is that this project will only look attractive if cash flows go beyond Troy's initial estimates (remember, each year there are salaries for the four new consultants and at some point you will need six such consultants). Given the statement concerning revenues reaching $10,000,000 after four years, some students will want to consider this project over a longer time horizon. Of course, the higher the estimates of cash flows, the more attractive the project.

This case is intended to show that projects are only as good as the estimates of cash flow. In addition, you may wish to ask the students about competitors and their potential impact on this project.

CHAPTER 13

Problem 13.1

    a. True
    b. True
    c. True
    d. True
    e. False
    f. False
    g. True

Problem 13.2

The objective of postauditing capital investments is threefold. First, postauditing provides a financial control mechanism, which facilitates corrective measures to an existing project. Second, postauditing provides input for future projects. Third, postauditing helps to overcome psychological and political problems associated with proposing and terminating projects.

The costs of postauditing capital investments relate to the time and effort involved in collecting and processing ex post information related to capital expenditures. The benefits relate to the improvements in existing projects, and the insight gained in regards to selecting future projects. In addition, postauditing helps a firm cut its losses in a timely fashion, which results in better risk management.

Problem 13.3

Postauditing capital assets in foreign subsidiaries poses several additional concerns, when compared to postauditing assets at home (in terms of the parent country). These concerns would include the following:

- The degree of asymmetric information between headquarters and managers in foreign subsidiaries may be exacerbated thereby effecting the degree of postauditing required.

- Political and economic risks may vary across countries, which could effect the best way to conduct, and utilize the results of postauditing.
- Cultural differences across countries may effect the degree and method for conducting postauditing.
- Foreign tax laws may effect the way postauditing results are interpreted.

Problem 13.4

A.   Postauditing is actually a means of gathering information to facilitate control. Since there are costs and benefits to this activity, the information economics perspective is directly applicable (i.e., the benefits need to be compared to the costs of gathering such information).

B.   Large capital investments will, ceteris paribus, have more dollar benefits associated with good control (i.e., postauditing) than small capital investments. In fact, these benefits will likely be linearly related to the size of the capital project. The costs of postauditing, however, are not likely to be linearly related to the size of the capital project. Thus, on the surface, it would appear that large capital projects should be more frequently postaudited than small projects.

Problem 13.5

$$PV = \sum_{t=1}^{28} \frac{\$400,000}{(1+.15)^t} = \$2,613,403$$

$$AV = \$2,500,000$$

PV > AV, so the decision should be not to abandon Laur 23.

Problem 13.6

A. Asymmetric information refers to a situation where the agent has information that is not available to the principal. In the context of the relationship between postauditing and firm performance, Gordon and Smith showed that asymmetric information increased the potential performance benefits from postauditing. In multinational corporations, subunits (be it divisions or subsidiaries) are physically further apart. As Gordon and Smith showed, this physical separation led to greater asymmetric information. However, on-site postaudits of capital investments are more costly and logistically more difficult to carry out in a multinational organization. Thus, whereas postaudits may be more valuable in a multinational environment, they are also more costly and more difficult to implement.

B. The special concerns relating to postauditing a globally, vs. non-globally, oriented non-profit organization would be similar to those in a profit oriented corporation. More to the point, asymmetric information would be greater in a global environment and thus the potential value of such postaudits would be greater. However, the costs and difficulty associated with implementing postaudits would also be exacerbated.

Problem 13.7

$$AV = \$5,000,000$$

$$PV = \sum_{t=1}^{t} = \frac{\$1,500,000}{(1+.10)^t} - \$2,000,000$$

$$= \$5,686,180 - \$2,000,000$$

$$= \$3,686,180$$

Since $PV < AV$, abandon project.

CHAPTER 14

Problem 14.1

    a.   True
    b.   False
    c.   True
    d.   True
    e.   True
    f.   True
    g.   True

Problem 14.2

A.   Organizational change is actually structural change, which itself occurs whenever the interaction patterns of individuals within the organization change. The sending and receiving of information causes such change to take place.

B.   One type of organizational change taking place in the global marketplace is the use of new performance measures. Another type of change taking place is the use of new cost allocation schemes. In both cases, these changes create changes in interaction patterns among organizational members and in turn structural change.

Problem 14.3

The MAS is an integral part of an organization. Thus it becomes a moot issue as to which comes first. Indeed, the paper by Gordon and Narayanon (1984), as well as many subsequent studies, clearly show that organizational design issues and MAS design issues are best viewed as moving in tandem with each other.

Problem 14.4

Some organizations operate in rapidly changing (i.e., dynamic) environments, whereas others operate in relatively stable environments. However, even in relatively stable environments, change does occur. All one has to do is to look at the developments related to the Internet over the past decade to see this latter point. The Internet has caused changes, to one degree or another, in every organization. An organization's ability to adopt to such changes is the only way it will prevent itself from ultimately becoming obsolete.

As argued in this chapter, management accounting systems can act as agents of organizational change. For example, if an organization decides that its goal is to sell more of its products (including service oriented products) over the Internet, the management accounting system could easily derive and report the percentage of monthly (or weekly) sales that occur via this mode of transaction. The collection and reporting of such data on a product (or product line) basis will undoubtedly motivate managers to increase the percentage of Internet sales.

Problem 14.5

The MAS could provide:

1. The firm's growth rate related to industry's growth rate;
2. Global vs. domestic sales trends for the firm and the industry;
3. The industry's cost of capital vs. the firm's cost of capital;
4. Capital investment spending trends for the firm vs. the industry;
5. Research and development spending for the firm vs. the industry.

Problem 14.6

A. At least four advantages of planning through brainstorming sessions include:

- Ideas which are valuable and often better in quality than those generated separately, as one idea leads to another or pieces of one combine with another;

- Using other people for ideas by bringing the talents of various individuals with different backgrounds together;
- Participation leading to more ideas which will give rise to more alternatives;
- Clustering of ideas before evaluation, i.e., short improvements, capital requirements, employee knowledge, attitudes, etc.

B.   At least four advantages of formal organizational planning include:

- Providing structure to the company, assigning responsibilities, and focusing energy and efforts. A chain of command is in place.
- Encouraging an analysis of the organization's environment, i.e., concepts of market and technology translated into specific products, estimates of product demand, and governmental impacts.
- Encouraging analyses of organizational strengths and weaknesses, i.e., product and market capabilities, production capacity, technical skills, organizational structure, and human resources.
- Generating, evaluating, and selecting alternative strategies in order to take advantage of opportunities.

C.   At least three reasons why the management group of Bio-Cure Inc. is likely to resist change in the planning technique include:

- A general feeling that the plan is imposed by outsiders which could lead to anger, fear, and mistrust;.
- Displeasure, as the imposed plan may stymie the flexibility and creativity that apparently existed before, particularly from a scientific-oriented research group;
- A change in organizational culture.

D.   At least two ways that communication could have been improved, thereby making the change in planning technique more acceptable to Bio-Cure Inc.'s management group include:

- The president of the venture capital group calling a meeting of everyone to explain the overriding organizational, functional, and integration strategies and that planning is a dynamic process requiring revision as new information is developed;
- Encouraging feedback and participation from the managers responsible for implementing the plans.

Problem 14.7

A.   The organizational structures depicted by the two charts are the product line and functional organizational structures, respectively. The current structure is a product line organization. In this structure, the accounting managers have a dual reporting role as in a matrix structure. The proposed structure is a functional organization alignment.

B.

    1.   At least two advantages and two disadvantages of the current (product line) organizational structure include the following:

    Advantages

- Faster product decisions;
- Functional support dedicated to operations thereby reducing conflicts. The Vice President of each product has control over all facets of the product line.

    Disadvantages

- A more complex management structure with a broader span of control;
- The decentralization of accounting with multiple supervisors and dual reporting.

    2.   At least two advantages and two disadvantages of the proposed (functional) organizational structure include the following:

    Advantages

- Specialized top management exerting more control with a unified objective approach;
- The reduction of duplication of support specialization where economies of scale can be achieved.

    Disadvantages

- Less opportunity for the development of general corporate management personnel;

- Less overall results orientation with more focus on functional objectives than product profitability.

C.   The circumstances that would favor the current product line structure include:

- A large organization with diverse product lines and markets;
- A large pool of employees possessing the desired or specialized management skills.

The circumstances that would favor the proposed functional structure include:

- A small organization with a limited number of product lines;
- Common markets and technology.